Ravenscourt
B·O·O·K·S
Teacher's Guide

Overcoming Adversity

Books 1-8

The Last Boat
Inspiring Excellence
Playing through Pain
Once There Were Two
Walls of Water
Robinson Crusoe
Alice in Wonderland
Monte Cristo's Prison Years

McGraw Hill SRA

Columbus, OH

SRAonline.com

McGraw Hill SRA

Copyright © 2008 by SRA/McGraw-Hill.

All rights reserved. No part of this publication may be reproduced or distributed in any form or by any means, or stored in a database or retrieval system, without the prior written consent of The McGraw-Hill Companies, Inc., including, but not limited to, network storage or transmission, or broadcast for distance learning.

Printed in the United States of America.

Send all inquiries to this address:
SRA/McGraw-Hill
4400 Easton Commons
Columbus, OH 43219

ISBN: 978-0-07-611315-6
MHID: 0-07-611315-9

3 4 5 6 7 8 9 MAL 13 12 11 10 09 08

The McGraw-Hill Companies

Table of Contents

Ravenscourt Books 1
Reading and Fluency 2
Using *Ravenscourt Books* 3
Individual Progress Chart 8
Fluency Graph 9
Book Summaries 10
The Last Boat 12
    Answer Key 22
Inspiring Excellence 24
    Answer Key 34
Playing through Pain 36
    Answer Key 46
Once There Were Two 48
    Answer Key 58
Walls of Water 60
    Answer Key 70
Robinson Crusoe 72
    Answer Key 82
Alice in Wonderland 84
    Answer Key 94
Monte Cristo's Prison Years 96
    Answer Key 106
Graphic Organizers 108

Ravenscourt Books

Placing Students

Written for middle school to young adult readers, *Ravenscourt Books* provides materials and activities for enhancing the comprehension and fluency of struggling readers. Each of these fiction and nonfiction selections is

- organized within themes that are both engaging and informative.
- built to provide students with additional opportunities to read independently.
- designed to provide frequent opportunities for reading to improve fluency and overall reading achievement.

Some teachers have found these selections align with the independent reading levels of students in the *Corrective Reading* program. Use the chart below to place your students in the appropriate set of *Ravenscourt Readers.*

	For students who have successfully completed	Reading level	Page count (average number of words per book)
Getting Started	Corrective Reading Decoding A*	1	28 (800)
Discovery	Corrective Reading Comprehension A*	2	28 (1,800)
Anything's Possible	Corrective Reading Decoding B1*	2	28 (1,800)
The Unexpected	Corrective Reading Comprehension B1*	2	28 (1,800)
Express Yourself	Corrective Reading Decoding B2*	3	44 (4,200)
Overcoming Adversity	Corrective Reading Comprehension B2*	3	44 (4,200)
Moving Forward	Corrective Reading Decoding C* Lesson 60	5	60 (7,500)
Reaching Goals	Corrective Reading Comprehension C* Lesson 60	5	60 (7,500)

*or have attained comparable skills

Components

The **Using *Ravenscourt Books*** section explains how to incorporate these components into an effective supplemental reading program.

Chapter Books
- Include eight age-appropriate books in each set
- Feature fiction, nonfiction, and retold classics
- Present additional practice for essential vocabulary and decoding skills
- Provide fast-moving story lines for independent reading

Fluency Audio CDs
- Model pronunciation, phrasing, intonation, and expression
- Assist students in improving their oral-reading fluency

Evaluation and Tracking Software
- Motivates students by delivering activities electronically
- Scores, records, and tracks student progress

Teacher's Guides
- Outline ways to use the series in your classroom
- Include comprehension activities, word lists, and fluency practice
- Provide prereading activities and postreading writing activities
- Address reading and language arts standards

Online Support

Go to **SRAonline.com** and click on *Ravenscourt Books* for additional support and materials.

Overcoming Adversity

Reading and Fluency

Reading

Reading is not simply decoding or word recognition; it is understanding the text. Students who read slowly or hesitantly are not able to concentrate on meaning.

Fluency

Fluency bridges the gap between decoding and comprehension and characterizes proficient reading. Increased oral-reading fluency improves reading comprehension.

Fluent and Nonfluent Readers

The chart below presents an easy way to compare fluent and nonfluent readers. If students have several of the listed characteristics of nonfluent readers, refer to the sections on *Assessing Fluency* and *Fluency Practice* in the **Using *Ravenscourt Books*** section that begins on page 3.

A Fluent Reader	A Nonfluent Reader
Reads words accurately	Reads with omissions, pauses, mispronunciations, insertions, and substitutions
Decodes automatically	Reverses word order
Reads smoothly	Reads word-by-word, focusing on words
Reads at an appropriate rate	Reads slowly, hesitantly
Reads with expression and phrasing	Reads without expression; ignores punctuation
Reads with understanding of text	Reads with limited comprehension
Reads so text sounds like speech	Reads without natural intonation

Oral-Reading Fluency

Oral-reading fluency is the ability to read accurately, at an appropriate rate, and with good expression and phrasing. The foundation for oral-reading fluency is automatic word recognition and extensive practice with materials that are easy for the students to read.

Oral-reading fluency develops as a result of multiple opportunities to practice reading successfully. The primary strategy for developing oral-reading fluency is to provide extensive and frequent opportunities for students to read text with high levels of accuracy. This means that selected passages should be ones the students are able to read with at least 95 percent accuracy.

Repeated and monitored oral reading is an effective intervention strategy for students who do not read fluently. By reading the same passage a number of times, students become familiar with the words it contains and recognize the words automatically. This improves reading fluency and overall reading achievement. It also builds confidence and motivation—particularly when students chart their progress.

The minimum target oral-reading fluency rate is 60 *words read correctly per minute* (wcpm) for **Getting Started** and **Discovery,** 90 wcpm for **Anything's Possible** and **The Unexpected,** 130 wcpm for **Express Yourself** and **Overcoming Adversity,** and 150 wcpm for **Moving Forward** and **Reaching Goals.**

How to assess fluency, how to set realistic target rates, and how to practice fluency will be discussed in greater detail in the **Using *Ravenscourt Books*** section.

Using *Ravenscourt Books*

Grouping

Students who have completed *Comprehension B2* will have mastered the decoding skills and vocabulary necessary to independently read the stories in **Overcoming Adversity.**

Ravenscourt Books may be taught to the whole class, small groups, or pairs. Assign each student to a partner. Partners can do paired readings for fluency practice. The partners will read the same story at the same time. *Ravenscourt Books* may also be used for individual student reading.

Scheduling

Ravenscourt Books is intended to be used as a supplement to your core program and should be scheduled in addition to the regular lessons. Times to use the books include

- reading and language arts blocks,
- before- and after-school programs,
- summer school,
- and out-of-school reading with parental support.

A Suggested Lesson Plan for *Ravenscourt Books*	
Part 1	1) Introduce the series, and help students select a book. 2) Assess students' initial oral-reading fluency by completing a "cold read" of one of the book's fluency passages. The **Fluency Passage** section can be found after the **Thinking and Writing** section for each book. (See *Assessing Fluency* on page 4.) 3) Have students complete the **Building Background** activities.
Part 2	1) Preteach the unfamiliar words for the first chapter in the **Word Lists** section of the *Teacher's Guide* for each book. 2) Have students read the title of the first chapter aloud. 3) Have students listen to a fluent reader read the first chapter as they follow along with the text. 4) Have student pairs take turns reading the chapter again. 5) Have students take the **Chapter Quiz.** 6) Have some students do repeated readings to improve oral-reading fluency. 7) Repeat Part 2 for subsequent chapters.
Part 3	1) Have students complete the **Thinking and Writing** section. 2) Take fluency scores, using the same fluency passage used in Part 1. Have students enter their scores on their **Fluency Graph.**

Selecting Books

The books in each set are leveled so students can start with any book in the set. However, students generally find contemporary fiction easier to read than nonfiction and retold classics.

On pages 10–11 you will find **Book Summaries** that give a brief outline of each book.

- If the book is a retold classic, information about the original author is included.
- If the book is a good tool for teaching a literary term, the term is explained. The teacher should teach the term before the students begin reading.
- The last section includes other resources—books, films, or Web sites—that contain related information. These resources can be used for extra credit, reports, projects, and so on. Evaluate all books, films, and Web sites to confirm appropriateness of the content prior to sharing these materials with students.

Using Ravenscourt Books

Introducing the Series

1. Write the series theme on the board.
   - Tell the students that the books in the set all relate in some way to this common theme.
   - Brainstorm ideas about the theme, and write the students' ideas on a large sheet of chart paper. Include words, topics, and types of stories related to the theme. Post this list for student reference.
2. The books in each set represent several genres—fiction, nonfiction, biography, science fiction, historical fiction, retold classics, and so on.
   - Ask the students to read the title and the summary on the back of the book they chose.
   - Have the students predict how their book relates to the theme.
   - If the book is nonfiction, ask the student to predict what kinds of questions it could answer.

Whole-Class Instruction

The following sections are designed for whole-class instruction but may be modified for small groups or individual instruction.

Set up classes in the *Evaluation and Tracking Software,* or make a copy of the **Individual Progress Chart** for each student.

Assessing Fluency

Make a class set of copies of the **Fluency Graph** on page 9 of the *Teacher's Guide.* Follow these steps to **ASSESS STUDENTS' INITIAL ORAL-READING FLUENCY.**

1. Have the student read a passage that is set at the appropriate length (60–150 words) and at the appropriate instructional reading level (at least 95 percent accuracy).
   - The **Fluency Passage** section can be found after the **Thinking and Writing** section for each book.
2. Ask the student to do a one-minute reading of the unrehearsed passage.
3. Ask the student whether she or he is ready.
   - Then say: **Please begin.**
4. Follow along as the student reads.
   - When an error occurs, mark the error.
   - Count the following as errors: mispronunciations, omissions, substitutions, insertions, and failure to identify a word within three seconds.
   - Don't mark words the student self-corrects.
   - Don't mark off for proper nouns.
5. At the end of one minute, make a vertical line on the page after the last word read.
6. Count the number of words up to the last word read.
7. Subtract the number of errors to determine the wcpm.
8. Enter the number of words read correctly on the student's **Fluency Graph** by filling in the column to the appropriate number.
9. At the bottom of the graph, circle the number of errors made.
10. Review any words the student missed and provide practice on those words. The minimum goals for fluency are the following:
    - The goal for students who have completed *Decoding A* or have equivalent skills is to read the books in **Getting Started** at a minimum rate of 60 wcpm.
    - The goal for students who have completed *Comprehension A* or have equivalent skills is to read the books in **Discovery** at a minimum rate of 60 wcpm.
    - The goal for students who have completed *Decoding B1* or have equivalent skills is to read the books in **Anything's Possible** at a minimum rate of 90 wcpm.
    - The goal for students who have completed *Comprehension B1* or have equivalent skills is to read the books in **The Unexpected** at a minimum rate of 90 wcpm.

Using Ravenscourt Books

- The goal for students who have completed *Decoding B2* or have equivalent skills is to read the books in **Express Yourself** at a minimum rate of 130 wcpm.
- The goal for students who have completed *Comprehension B2* or have equivalent skills is to read the books in **Overcoming Adversity** at a minimum rate of 130 wcpm.
- The goal for students who have completed Lesson 60 of *Decoding C* or have equivalent skills is to read the books in **Moving Forward** at a minimum rate of 150 wcpm.
- The goal for students who have completed Lesson 60 of *Comprehension C* or have equivalent skills is to read the books in **Reaching Goals** at a minimum rate of 150 wcpm.

Word Lists

Follow this procedure to preteach the words for each chapter of every book.

1. Provide students with a copy of the **Word Lists** page, or copy the words onto the board. Underline word parts if appropriate.
2. Begin with *Proper Nouns* by saying:
   - **These are the names of important people and places in Chapter 1.**
   - **Touch the first word in the column.**
   - Point to an underlined word part (if necessary) and say: **What sound?** (Signal.)
   - **What word?** (Signal.)
   - (Repeat until firm.)
3. For difficult and irregular words, say:
   - **Touch the word.**
   - **The word is _____.** (Signal.)
   - **What word?** (Signal.)
   - **Spell _____.** (Signal for each letter.)
   - **What word?** (Signal.)
   - (Repeat until firm.)
4. Follow the same procedure with *Unfamiliar Words*. Discuss the meanings of the words. Use the words in sentences as needed. The *Word Meanings* category is comprised of the words used in the *Word Meanings* section of **Building Background,** so some of the words may be familiar. Only use the following procedure for unfamiliar words.
   - Point to each unfamiliar word, say the word, and then say **What does _____ mean?** (Call on individual students.)
   - (Repeat until firm.)

Building Background

Use the **Building Background** section in the *Teacher's Guide* or on the *Evaluation and Tracking Software.* You can use this section as a whole-class activity or as an independent activity.

Whole-Class Activity

1. Divide the students into small groups. Hand out copies of the **Building Background** page for that book.
2. Read the questions in the *What You Know* section. Have the groups discuss the questions and write an answer for them. Have a member of each group read the group's answers to the class.
3. Read the words in the *Word Meanings* section.
   - Then read the directions and go over each question with the students and say, **Which word best answers this question?** (Call on individual students.)
   - Repeat this procedure for all of the words. (Note: If the directions indicate that the questions should be answered once the words have been introduced in the book, go over each word again after the students have read the word in context and have them answer the question associated with that word.)
4. Collect the papers and score them based on the number of correct answers. Refer to the **Answer Key** for each book.

Using Ravenscourt Books

Independent Activity

1. Hand out copies of the **Building Background** page. Have students take turns reading each question in the *What You Know* section. Have students write their answers before proceeding to the next question.
2. Have students read the words in the *Word Meanings* section. Then have them read the directions and complete the section.
   - When students are finished, collect the papers and score them based on completion and effort. Refer to the **Answer Key** for each book.

The teacher may enter the scores on the **Individual Progress Chart** found in the *Teacher's Guide* or on the *Evaluation and Tracking Software.*

Reading the Chapter

First, the students listen to a fluent reader read the chapter. The fluency model may be the teacher, a parent, a tutor, a teacher's aide, a peer, or the *Fluency Audio CDs.* Students read along, tracking the text with their fingers. Next, students take turns reading the chapter with their peer partner. An individual student reads aloud to the teacher, tutor, or parent, who gives feedback, points out missed words, and models, using punctuation, to improve expressive reading.

Chapter Quiz

After the second reading of the chapter, the student takes the **Chapter Quiz**. The quizzes have multiple-choice, true-or-false, sequence, and short-answer questions. The chapter quizzes are available on the *Evaluation and Tracking Software* or as blackline masters in the *Teacher's Guide.* Use the **Answer Keys** to score the blackline masters and enter scores on the **Individual Progress Chart** found on page 8. The *Evaluation and Tracking Software* will automatically grade and record the scores for all non-short-answer questions for each **Chapter Quiz**.

Students should take each quiz once and do their best the first time. Students must score a minimum of 80 percent to continue. If the student does not score 80 percent, he or she should reread the chapter before retaking the quiz.

Fluency Practice

Fluency practice improves comprehension. The teacher may choose different ways to practice fluency, depending on the student's needs. For students who are close to the target rate, have the student reread the whole chapter using one of these techniques:

- **Echo reading** A fluent reader reads a sentence aloud, and the student *echoes* it—repeats it with the same intonation and phrasing.
- **Unison or choral reading** A pair, group, or class reads a chapter aloud together.
- **Paired reading** The student reads a page aloud and receives feedback from his or her peer partner. Record the fluency scores on the **Fluency Graph** found in the *Teacher's Guide* or on the *Evaluation and Tracking Software.* Recording progress motivates student achievement.

For students who are significantly below the target rate, conduct **REPEATED READINGS TO IMPROVE ORAL-READING FLUENCY.** The student will reread the passages marked by asterisks in each of the books' chapters.

1. Set a target rate for the passage.
   - The target rate should be high enough to require the student to reread the passage several times.
   - A reasonable target rate is 40 percent higher than the baseline level.
   - For example, if the student initially reads the passage at a rate of 60 wcpm, the target rate for that passage would be 84 wcpm (**60** x .40 = 24; **60** + 24 = 84).

Using Ravenscourt Books

2. Have the student listen to the passage read fluently by a skilled reader or on the corresponding *Fluency Audio CD* while following along, pointing to the words as they are read.
3. After listening to the fluency model, have the student reread the same passage aloud for one minute.
   - A partner listens and records errors but does not interrupt the reader during the one-minute timed reading.
   - If the student makes more than six errors, he or she should listen to the fluency model again.
4. The student should read the same passage three to five times during the session or until the target rate is met, whichever comes first.
   - After each rereading, the student records the wcpm on his or her **Fluency Graph.**
   - If the target rate is not met, have the student read the same passage again the next day.
   - If the target rate is met, the student repeats the procedure with the next chapter.

Thinking and Writing

Many state assessments require students to produce extended writing about a story or an article they have read. Like **Building Background,** this section is not computer-scored and may be used in one of several ways. The *Think About It* section is intended to help students summarize what they have read and to relate the book to other books in the set, to the theme, or to the students' life experiences.

1. The questions in the *Think About It* section can be used for discussion.
   - Students discuss the questions in small groups and then write their individual responses on the blackline masters or using the *Evaluation and Tracking Software.*
   - The teacher may score the response using a variety of rubrics. For example, the teacher could give points for all reasonable responses in complete sentences that begin with a capital letter and end with appropriate punctuation.
2. For certain students, the teacher may ask the questions and prompt the student to give a thoughtful oral response.
3. Another option is to use *Think About It* as a mini-assessment. Have the students answer the questions independently on paper or using the *Evaluation and Tracking Software.*

The *Write About It* section gives students extended practice writing about what they have read. Students may write for as long as time allows.

The students may answer on the blackline master or use the *Evaluation and Tracking Software.* To motivate students, the *Evaluation and Tracking Software* includes a spelling checker and a variety of fonts and colors for students to choose from. This section is teacher-scored. Scores may be entered on a copy of the **Individual Progress Chart** or on the *Evaluation and Tracking Software.*

Students may keep their essays in a writing portfolio. At the end of the term students choose one of their essays to improve using the writing process. The final question in each *Write About It* section asks students to complete one of the graphic organizers that can be found as blackline masters in the back of this *Teacher's Guide* or on the *Evaluation and Tracking Software.* Graphic organizers are a structured, alternative writing experience. There are Book Report Forms, a What I Know/What I Learned Chart, a Sequencing Chart, and so on. Scores may be entered on the blackline master or *Evaluation and Tracking Software* version of the **Individual Progress Chart.**

Individual Progress Chart

- Enter the percentage correct score for each quiz or activity.

Book Title	Building Background	Chapter 1 Quiz	Chapter 2 Quiz	Chapter 3 Quiz	Chapter 4 Quiz	Chapter 5 Quiz	Chapter 6 Quiz	Thinking and Writing	Graphic Organizer
The Last Boat									
Inspiring Excellence									
Playing through Pain									
Once There Were Two									
Walls of Water									
Robinson Crusoe									
Alice in Wonderland									
Monte Cristo's Prison Years									

Name:

Class:

Overcoming Adversity

Fluency Graph

Name: _____ Class: _____

WCPM RATE
Number of words read correctly in one minute

1. Read a fluency passage for one minute. 2. Find the next open column. 3. Color the column to the number that shows how far you read.
4. Mark the number of errors in the chart at the bottom.

ERRORS (Above 6)

Fluency Graph

Overcoming Adversity

Book Summaries

The Last Boat
By Ilie Ruby

Summary
Luis thinks of himself as a loser. When his much-admired older brother is killed, Luis thinks it should have been him instead. When Luis's mother hears him talking about joining a gang, she sends him to stay with an aunt who lives near the ocean. Luis learns about himself as he learns to sail. Even though he finishes last in a race, he discovers that he isn't a loser after all.

Literary Terms
Simile: a comparison using *like* or *as*

Coming-of-Age Story: main character is initiated into adulthood through knowledge, experience, or both; changes may be from ignorance to knowledge, innocence to experience, false view of the world to correct view, idealism to realism, or immature responses to mature responses

Other Resources
Book: Adkins, Jan. *The Craft of Sail: A Primer of Sailing* (Walker and Company, 1994)

Movies: *Wind* (1992); *White Squall* (1996); *Learn to Sail* (1999)

Web sites: http://www.ussailing.org/
http://www.cccturtle.org/kemps.htm

Inspiring Excellence
By Elizabeth Laskey

Summary
The author describes the origins of the Paralympics, a sporting event held once every four years for athletes who are physically disabled. Since the first Paralympics in 1960, the event has grown to become the second largest athletic event in the world. Only the Olympics exceed them. Following the information about the Paralympics are five inspiring biographies of famous and well-respected Paralympic athletes. Each overcame seemingly overwhelming obstacles to become the best at what they do.

Literary Terms
Nonfiction: a factual piece of literature

Biography: an account of a person's life written by another person

Other Resources
Book: Philbrick, Rodman. *Freak the Mighty* (Scholastic, Reissue edition, 1995)

Web sites: http://www.paralympic.org/release/Main_Sections_Menu/index.html
http://www.usoc.org/paralympics/

Playing through Pain
By Barbara Wood

Summary
Roberto Clemente is one of the greatest legends in the history of baseball. Clemente was born to play baseball, and he loved it from the start. Clemente paved the way for other Latino baseball players. He showed courage because he played baseball in spite of poverty, physical injury, chronic health problems, and ethnic prejudice. Sadly, Clemente died at a young age. Clemente is remembered as a great ballplayer and a great humanitarian.

Literary Term
Biography: an account of a person's life written by another person

Other Resources
Books: Dunham, Montrew and Meryl Henderson. *Roberto Clemente: Young Ball Player* (Aladdin Library, 1997); Kingsbury, Robert. *Roberto Clemente* (Rosen Publishing Group, 2003); Wagenheim, Kal and Wilfrid Sheed. *Clemente!* (Olmstead Press, 2001)

Movies: *Roberto Clemente* (1993); *Roberto Clemente—A Video Tribute* (1997, in Spanish)

Web site: http://www.robertoclemente.si.edu/

Once There Were Two
By Carole Gerber

Summary
Major league baseball once had a very different look. It wasn't the uniforms; it was the players. There were no African American players on the field. Segregation kept them in their own league. But what a league it was! Many of baseball's all-time great players played in the Negro Leagues. When Jackie Robinson broke the baseball color barrier in 1947, it was a great step for African Americans. Yet this was the beginning of the end for the Negro Leagues. Segregation is a part of U.S. history that some would like to forget. But one thing should never be forgotten—the great players of the Negro Leagues.

Literary Term
Nonfiction: a factual piece of literature

Other Resources
Book: McKissack, Patricia, et al. *Black Diamond: The Story of the Negro Baseball Leagues* (Polaris, 1998)

Movies: *Only the Ball Was White* (1993); *The Bingo Long Traveling All-Stars and Motor Kings* (1976); *Soul of the Game* (1996); *Baseball—A Film by Ken Burns* (1994)

Web sites: http://www.negroleaguebaseball.com/
http://www.nlbpa.com

Book Summaries

Walls of Water
By Susan Blackaby

Summary
In 1889 a dam broke and a wall of water roared into Johnstown, Pennsylvania. More than 100 years later, the Great Flood of 1993 devastated large areas in the Mississippi River Basin. Things had changed in 100 years. In 1889 more than 2,000 people lost their lives. In the Great Flood of 1993 only 48 people died. In the century between the two disasters, flood watchers learned how to predict flooding, to warn people, and to protect property.

Literary Terms
Nonfiction: a factual piece of literature
Foreshadowing: an author's hints about events that will occur later in the story

Other Resources
Book: Walker, Paul Robert. *Head for the Hills! The Amazing True Story of the Johnstown Flood* (Random House, 1993)
Movies: *20th Century with Mike Wallace—Underwater: The Great Flood of '93* (1999); *Untamed Earth: Ferocious Floods* (2003); *Johnstown Flood DVD* (2003)
Web site: http://www.johnstownpa.com/History/hist30.html

Robinson Crusoe
Retold by Carole Gerber

Summary
As a young man, Robinson Crusoe ignored his family when they told him not to go to sea. He soon found himself shipwrecked on a deserted island. Crusoe taught himself how to survive and lived on the island for nearly 28 years. During that time he discovered what mattered to him in life.

Authors
Daniel Defoe worked as a journalist and a novelist. *Robinson Crusoe* was based on the experiences of a real person.

Literary Terms
Foreshadowing: an author's hints about events that will occur later in the story
Adventure: realistic characters and events; emphasizes action and suspense; setting is a real place or a place that could be real; sometimes includes a chase or attempt to find some object or reach a specific goal

Other Resources
Book: Defoe, Daniel. *Robinson Crusoe.* Abridged by Robert Blaisdell, et al. (Dover Publications, 1995)
Movies: *Robinson Crusoe* (1996); *Cast Away* (2001)
Web site: http://www.online-literature.com/defoe/crusoe

Alice in Wonderland
Retold by Hilary Mac Austin

Summary
Alice, bored with reading, falls asleep under a tree and is awakened by a talking rabbit. After following the rabbit down a hole, she ends up in a curious place where she encounters talking animals, crazy characters and magical potions. After playing a bizarre game of croquet, she watches a nonsense trial and is attacked by a deck of cards. Will she ever make it out of this topsy-turvy world?

Author
Alice's Adventures in Wonderland was originally written by Lewis Carroll (1832–1898), an English author. Carroll wrote the stories for Alice Liddell, the daughter of a friend. Published in 1865, the stories were instantly popular with children and later became popular with adults due to their clever mix of themes and elements.

Literary Terms
Setting: the story's environment; its time and place
Suspense: arousing the reader's curiosity or making the reader wonder what will happen next

Other Resources
Book: Barrie, J. M. and Elisa Trimby. *Peter Pan* (Puffin, 2002)
Movie: *Alice in Wonderland* (Disney, 1951)
Web site: http://www.online-literature.com/carroll/alice/

Monte Cristo's Prison Years
Retold by Linda Lott

Summary
Edmond Dantès was a happy man until he was unjustly imprisoned. Dantès was thrown into the dungeon. One night he heard the scratching sounds of someone trying to escape. This was Abbot Faria, who told Dantès of a treasure. Can Dantès escape to find the treasure?

Author
Alexandre Dumas lived an exciting life, so it is no wonder that he wrote such interesting books. Another of his books is *The Three Musketeers*.

Literary Terms
Suspense: arousing the reader's curiosity or making the reader wonder what will happen next
Irony: the difference between the expected results of a situation and the actual results

Other Resources
Book: Dumas, Alexandre. *The Count of Monte Cristo.* Translated and abridged by Lowell Bair. (Bantam Classic Edition, 1981)
Movie: *The Count of Monte Cristo* (2002)
Web site: http://www.online-literature.com/dumas/cristo/

Overcoming Adversity

Building Background

Name _____ Date _____

The Last Boat
What You Know

Write answers to these questions.

1. Find out more about small sailboats. How are they propelled and controlled? How does the sail work with the wind?

   _____
   _____

2. Have you ever been in a race? What did you experience before and after the race began? Did you race with a team or as an individual?

   _____
   _____

3. What do you think is most difficult when learning a new skill or sport?

   _____
   _____

4. What steps do you think people can take to help protect animals that are on the endangered list? _____
   _____

Word Meanings
Definitions
Look for these words as you read your chapter book. When you find one of these words, write its definition.

capsize: _____

current: _____

endangered: _____

instinct: _____

navigate: _____

spinnaker: _____

12   Overcoming Adversity • Book 1

Word Lists

The Last Boat

Unfamiliar Words	Word Meanings	Proper Nouns	
attitude pilot promise	instinct	Auntie Boom Luis New York City Ruben Ray	Chapter 1
dangerous erosion expensive leather loyalty marina pontoon restaurants rickety whether yacht	current endangered	Atlantic Ocean Beulah MacDuff Cape Fear River Commodore's Regatta George Zamora Independence Day Roberto Victorian	Chapter 2
condition hatchlings loggerhead		Gulf of Mexico Kemp's ridley turtle Oak Island Stumpy	Chapter 3
challenge commercial frothing identify obvious pathetic patience precision technique trophy	capsize navigate spinnaker		Chapter 4
criticizes			Chapter 5
			Chapter 6

Overcoming Adversity • Book 1   13

Chapter Quiz

Name _____ Date _____

The Last Boat
Chapter 1, "Lost Summer"

Fill in the bubble beside the answer for each question.

1. What did Mama make the boys promise?
   - Ⓐ They would not get into trouble.
   - Ⓑ They would do all their chores.
   - Ⓒ They would not go near water.

2. What did Mama try to do in the summer?
   - Ⓐ make the boys join a club
   - Ⓑ make the boys find a job
   - Ⓒ make the boys stay indoors

3. How was Luis like his father?
   - Ⓐ He did things his own way.
   - Ⓑ He wanted to be a pilot.
   - Ⓒ He had the same brown eyes.

4. Where did Mama send Luis?
   - Ⓐ to his aunt's house
   - Ⓑ to summer camp
   - Ⓒ to his room

Read the question, and write your answer.

How did Luis's father die? _____

_____

_____

Chapter Quiz

Name _____ Date _____

The Last Boat
Chapter 2, "The River of Fear"

Mark each statement *T* for true or *F* for false.

____ 1. Auntie Boom is not very talkative.

____ 2. Auntie Boom asks Luis to look at things closely.

____ 3. Luis misses his life in the city.

____ 4. Auntie Boom has always saved things, and she promised to save Luis.

____ 5. Luis answers all of Auntie Boom's questions.

____ 6. Luis had never been to the beach before.

____ 7. Auntie Boom doesn't know very much about nature.

____ 8. "Boom" is named for her laughter that shakes windows like thunder.

____ 9. Luis is looking forward to learning to sail.

____ 10. To spite Auntie Boom, Luis didn't eat breakfast.

Read the question, and write your answer.

What kinds of things does Aunt Boom try to teach Luis about Cape Fear and the surrounding area? _____

_____

_____

Overcoming Adversity • Book 1

Chapter Quiz

Name _____ Date _____

The Last Boat
Chapter 3, "Escape!"

Fill in the bubble beside the answer for each question.

1. Why did Luis want Auntie Boom to go to sleep?
   - Ⓐ so he could go to sleep
   - Ⓑ so he could escape
   - Ⓒ so he could find his sneakers

2. What happened to the turtle nest?
   - Ⓐ Roberto fell on it.
   - Ⓑ Luis rode his bike over it.
   - Ⓒ Foxes attacked it.

3. Why did the boys move away to fight?
   - Ⓐ to keep from hurting the eggs
   - Ⓑ to get down from the dune
   - Ⓒ to get away from the water

4. What is Roberto's secret?
   - Ⓐ He stole Luis's sneakers.
   - Ⓑ He takes care of the turtle eggs.
   - Ⓒ He hates sailing.

Read the question, and write your answer.

Describe Stumpy and explain why she is important. _____

_____

_____

Chapter Quiz

Name _____ Date _____

The Last Boat
Chapter 4, "Sailing"

Number the events in order from 1 to 5.

___ George gives Luis warning number 1.

___ George teaches Luis and four others the parts of a sailboat.

___ Luis loses control of the boat and stalls it on a sandbar.

___ Luis unties his boat and glides away.

___ George tows the boats around the harbor to show the sailors the rocks.

Mark each statement *T* for true or *F* for false.

___ 1. Luis learns that knots are a way to measure speed and are also in ropes.

___ 2. Luis pays close attention to George as he discusses his equipment.

___ 3. A *regatta* is big triangular sail that makes the boat go fast.

___ 4. Luis challenges the ferryboat with his sailboat.

___ 5. George says Luis fights the wind and the river.

Read the question, and write your answer.

Why do you think Luis challenges the ferryboat in his little sailboat?

_____

_____

_____

Overcoming Adversity • Book 1

Chapter Quiz

Name _____ Date _____

The Last Boat
Chapter 5, "Righting the Boat"

Mark each statement *T* for true or *F* for false.

_____ 1. Auntie Boom tries to show Luis how to use the wind and the water.

_____ 2. Roberto teaches Luis how to right the boat.

_____ 3. Luis is happy to see Roberto.

_____ 4. Roberto makes Luis capsize the boat on purpose.

_____ 5. Luis follows Roberto's steps exactly.

_____ 6. Luis's way of righting the boat works just as well.

_____ 7. Luis wants to race in the regatta.

_____ 8. Roberto gives back Luis's sneakers.

_____ 9. The sneakers are as good as new.

_____ 10. George tells Luis not to join the race.

Read the question, and write your answer.

What do you think will happen in the next chapter? _____
_____
_____

Chapter Quiz

Name _____ Date _____

The Last Boat
Chapter 6, "The Last Boat In"

Number the events in order from 1 to 5.

____ A boat headed towards Luis.

____ Luis righted the boat and saved himself.

____ Wind and rain whipped up and Luis's boat capsized.

____ Luis decided to enter the race.

____ Luis remembered Roberto's steps.

Mark each statement *T* for true or *F* for false.

____ 1. Luis is ashamed of his sailing skills.

____ 2. Luis and Auntie Boom watch Roberto race.

____ 3. Auntie Boom and Luis stay away from the dunes.

____ 4. Stumpy lays new eggs.

____ 5. Luis moves the eggs to a safe place.

Read the question, and write your answer.

Why do you think Luis decides to help protect the sea turtle eggs?

_____

_____

_____

Overcoming Adversity • Book 1

Thinking and Writing

Name _____ Date _____

The Last Boat
Think About It

Write about or give an oral presentation for each question.

1. Why was the summertime hard for Luis? _____

2. Was Mama right to send Luis away? Why or why not? _____

3. Why do you think Luis comes out a winner, even though he loses the race? _____

Write About It

Choose one of the questions below. Write your answer on a sheet of paper.

1. What was Luis's attitude at the beginning of the summer? How does it change? What difference will his new attitude make when he goes home?

2. Auntie Boom and Roberto loved nature. Luis learned to pay attention to things in nature. Why is it important to protect and respect nature?

3. A *simile* is a comparison using *like* or *as*. Find five similes in the story, and explain them.

4. Complete the Book Report Form for this book.

Fluency Passages

The Last Boat

Chapter 1 *pages 4 and 5*

*I was trouble, a volcano ready to erupt. Trouble found me	11
everywhere. I was smarter than most folks. I tried to do what I was	25
supposed to, but I never could.	31
"Luis, I'm not playing!" Mama would holler. She'd wave her long,	42
skinny finger at me. "You don't think. You stop fighting or else." But I	56
wasn't going to sit back and just take it like Ruben did. What good did	71
thinking do him?	74
I had the "fighting instinct" like my father. He had died in the war	88
when I was two. At least that's what we always said. But there was no real	104
war when our father was in army pilot training. He had decided to fly	118
through a storm. He flew with ice on the wings of his* plane. He did things	134
his own way.	137

Chapter 6 *page 42*

*Stay steady! I know how to talk to the wind. Don't fight. I turn the	15
rudder and pull in the sail. Whew!	22
One boat is leading. Another boat is struggling as it heads toward me.	35
I turn, but my sail falls. I switch sides.	44
Wind whips my boat. The rain beats the river. When my boat capsizes,	57
I know it's over. The wind flips the boat on top of me. I try to use my	75
weight to turn it over, but I'm sinking. Roberto righted my boat before,	88
not me. It's clear I'm defeated. Don't I know that I can trust myself?	102
No one sees me. No one can hear me. The Cape Fear River is	116
thundering. Just follow the steps. One at a time.	125
I right the boat and* save myself.	132

- The target rate for **Overcoming Adversity** is 130 wcpm. The asterisks (*) mark 130 words.
- Listen to the student read the passage. Count the number of words read in one minute and the number of errors.
- For the reading rate, subtract the number of errors from the total number of words read.
- Have students enter their scores on their **Fluency Graph.** See page 9.

Answer Key

Building Background

Name _____ Date _____

The Last Boat
What You Know
Write answers to these questions.

1. Find out more about small sailboats. How are they propelled and controlled? How does the sail work with the wind?
   the wind with the sail controls the speed of the boat; the rudder controls the direction; rudder and sail work together

2. Have you ever been in a race? What did you experience before and after the race began? Did you race with a team or as an individual?
   Answers will vary.

3. What do you think is most difficult when learning a new skill or sport?
   Ideas: getting familiar with the rules; getting better at using the new skill

4. What steps do you think people can take to help protect animals that are on the endangered list? **Ideas: take care of the animals' young; protect the areas the animals live in**

Word Meanings
Definitions
Look for these words as you read your chapter book. When you find one of these words, write its definition.

capsize: **to turn over or upset**
current: **a flow of water or air in a certain direction**
endangered: **put in danger or peril**
instinct: **a way of behaving that is natural to an animal or person from birth**
navigate: **to steer, or control the course of**
spinnaker: **a large triangular sail set on a long, light pole and used when sailing with the wind pushing from behind or nearly so**

12   Overcoming Adversity • Book 1

The Last Boat

Chapter Quiz

Name _____ Date _____

The Last Boat
Chapter 1, "Lost Summer"
Fill in the bubble beside the answer for each question.

1. What did Mama make the boys promise?
   ● They would not get into trouble.
   Ⓑ They would do all their chores.
   Ⓒ They would not go near water.

2. What did Mama try to do in the summer?
   Ⓐ make the boys join a club
   Ⓑ make the boys find a job
   ● make the boys stay indoors

3. How was Luis like his father?
   ● He did things his own way.
   Ⓑ He wanted to be a pilot.
   Ⓒ He had the same brown eyes.

4. Where did Mama send Luis?
   ● to his aunt's house
   Ⓑ to summer camp
   Ⓒ to his room

Read the question, and write your answer.

How did Luis's father die? **in a plane crash that occurred while he was flying through a storm**

14   Overcoming Adversity • Book 1

The Last Boat

Chapter Quiz

Name _____ Date _____

The Last Boat
Chapter 2, "The River of Fear"
Mark each statement *T* for true or *F* for false.

F 1. Auntie Boom is not very talkative.
T 2. Auntie Boom asks Luis to look at things closely.
T 3. Luis misses his life in the city.
T 4. Auntie Boom has always saved things, and she promised to save Luis.
F 5. Luis answers all of Auntie Boom's questions.
F 6. Luis had never been to the beach before.
F 7. Auntie Boom doesn't know very much about nature.
T 8. "Boom" is named for her laughter that shakes windows like thunder.
F 9. Luis is looking forward to learning to sail.
T 10. To spite Auntie Boom, Luis didn't eat breakfast.

Read the question, and write your answer.

What kinds of things does Aunt Boom try to teach Luis about Cape Fear and the surrounding area? **Ideas: about geology, history, nature**

Overcoming Adversity • Book 1   15

The Last Boat

Chapter Quiz

Name _____ Date _____

The Last Boat
Chapter 3, "Escape!"
Fill in the bubble beside the answer for each question.

1. Why did Luis want Auntie Boom to go to sleep?
   Ⓐ so he could go to sleep
   ● so he could escape
   Ⓒ so he could find his sneakers

2. What happened to the turtle nest?
   Ⓐ Roberto fell on it.
   Ⓑ Luis rode his bike over it.
   ● Foxes attacked it.

3. Why did the boys move away to fight?
   ● to keep from hurting the eggs
   Ⓑ to get down from the dune
   Ⓒ to get away from the water

4. What is Roberto's secret?
   Ⓐ He stole Luis's sneakers.
   ● He takes care of the turtle eggs.
   Ⓒ He hates sailing.

Read the question, and write your answer.

Describe Stumpy and explain why she is important. **Stumpy is a Kemp's ridley turtle, the most endangered type of sea turtle; Stumpy is missing a back flipper so she cannot bury her eggs to protect them from predators.**

16   Overcoming Adversity • Book 1

The Last Boat

Overcoming Adversity • Book 1

Answer Key

Chapter Quiz

Name _____ Date _____

The Last Boat
Chapter 4, "Sailing"

Number the events in order from 1 to 5.

- _5_ George gives Luis warning number 1.
- _1_ George teaches Luis and four others the parts of a sailboat.
- _4_ Luis loses control of the boat and stalls it on a sandbar.
- _3_ Luis unties his boat and glides away.
- _2_ George tows the boats around the harbor to show the sailors the rocks.

Mark each statement *T* for true or *F* for false.

- _T_ 1. Luis learns that knots are a way to measure speed and are also in ropes.
- _F_ 2. Luis pays close attention to George as he discusses his equipment.
- _F_ 3. A *regatta* is big triangular sail that makes the boat go fast.
- _T_ 4. Luis challenges the ferryboat with his sailboat.
- _T_ 5. George says Luis fights the wind and the river.

Read the question, and write your answer.

Why do you think Luis challenges the ferryboat in his little sailboat?
Ideas: to show he is not afraid; to prove he is a good sailor

The Last Boat — 17

Chapter Quiz

Name _____ Date _____

The Last Boat
Chapter 5, "Righting the Boat"

Mark each statement *T* for true or *F* for false.

- _T_ 1. Auntie Boom tries to show Luis how to use the wind and the water.
- _T_ 2. Roberto teaches Luis how to right the boat.
- _F_ 3. Luis is happy to see Roberto.
- _T_ 4. Roberto makes Luis capsize the boat on purpose.
- _F_ 5. Luis follows Roberto's steps exactly.
- _F_ 6. Luis's way of righting the boat works just as well.
- _F_ 7. Luis wants to race in the regatta.
- _T_ 8. Roberto gives back Luis's sneakers.
- _F_ 9. The sneakers are as good as new.
- _F_ 10. George tells Luis not to join the race.

Read the question, and write your answer.

What do you think will happen in the next chapter?
Accept reasonable responses.

The Last Boat — 18

Chapter Quiz

Name _____ Date _____

The Last Boat
Chapter 6, "The Last Boat In"

Number the events in order from 1 to 5.

- _2_ A boat headed towards Luis.
- _5_ Luis righted the boat and saved himself.
- _3_ Wind and rain whipped up and Luis's boat capsized.
- _1_ Luis decided to enter the race.
- _4_ Luis remembered Roberto's steps.

Mark each statement *T* for true or *F* for false.

- _F_ 1. Luis is ashamed of his sailing skills.
- _T_ 2. Luis and Auntie Boom watch Roberto race.
- _F_ 3. Auntie Boom and Luis stay away from the dunes.
- _T_ 4. Stumpy lays new eggs.
- _T_ 5. Luis moves the eggs to a safe place.

Read the question, and write your answer.

Why do you think Luis decides to help protect the sea turtle eggs?
Idea: he has learned to value nature, respect the environment, and help others

The Last Boat

Thinking and Writing

Name _____ Date _____

The Last Boat
Think About It

Write about or give an oral presentation for each question.

1. Why was the summertime hard for Luis? **Ideas: His brother had died in June; it was hot, and Mama wanted him to stay inside; he had no plans.**

2. Was Mama right to send Luis away? Why or why not? **Ideas: Yes, because the summer turned out well for Luis and he did not join the gang; no, because he missed his friends and his life in the city.**

3. Why do you think Luis comes out a winner, even though he loses the race? **Ideas: He learns a great deal; learns to follow directions; thinks clearly; helps the turtle**

Write About It

Choose one of the questions below. Write your answer on a sheet of paper.

1. What was Luis's attitude at the beginning of the summer? How does it change? What difference will his new attitude make when he goes home?

2. Auntie Boom and Roberto loved nature. Luis learned to pay attention to things in nature. Why is it important to protect and respect nature?

3. A *simile* is a comparison using *like* or *as*. Find five similes in the story, and explain them.

4. Complete the Book Report Form for this book.

The Last Boat

Overcoming Adversity • Book 1 — 23

Building Background

Name _____ Date _____

Inspiring Excellence
What You Know

Write answers to these questions.

1. What are the Olympics? Who takes part in the Olympics? Do you know any events that are similar to the Olympics? _____
   _____
   _____

2. What are some types of equipment that might help someone who cannot walk play a sport? _____
   _____

3. What does *persistence* mean? What does *excellence* mean? Do you think you can have excellence without persistence? Why or why not?
   _____
   _____

Word Meanings
Matching

Look for these words as you read your chapter book. When you find a word, draw a line to connect the word with the correct definition.

amputation	a competition in which the competitors are not restricted to a certain way of performing
artificial	a birth defect in which part of the spinal cord and its coverings are exposed through a gap in the backbone
bilateral	an operation to remove an arm or leg from the body
freestyle	a group of two or more arranged one behind the other
spina bifida	having or involving two sides or parties
tandem	made by a human being, not by nature

Word Lists

Inspiring Excellence

	Unfamiliar Words	Word Meanings	Proper Nouns	
Chapter 1	archery athletes cyclists equivalent fencing include injured parallel paralyzed physical skiing special	amputation	Dr. Ludwig Guttman [LOOD-vig GOOT-mun] Olympics Paralympics Stoke Mandeville Games	
Chapter 2	advocate famous machine raise	spina bifida	Chicago Marathon Ghana Illinois Jean Driscoll	
Chapter 3	accident adaptive competition extreme monoskier monoskiing waterskiing	freestyle	X Games	
Chapter 4	adopted amputee materials orphanage spokesperson	artificial	Australia Brian Frasure Bryan Hoddle Idaho Marlon Shirley Sydney	
Chapter 5		tandem	Braille Karissa Whitsell Matt Veatch Spencer Yates	
Chapter 6	completed medley promised pterygium syndrome [tuh-RIJ-ee-um] surgery triathlete triathlon	bilateral	Rudy Garcia-Tolson	

Chapter Quiz

Name _____ Date _____

Inspiring Excellence
Chapter 1, "The First Paralympics"

Fill in the bubble beside the answer for each question.

1. Who were the athletes in the first Stoke Mandeville Games?
   - Ⓐ soldiers who had injured their spinal cords in World War II
   - Ⓑ doctors and nurses at the Stoke Mandeville Hospital in England
   - Ⓒ good friends of Dr. Ludwig Guttman

2. What sports did athletes play at the first Stoke Mandeville Games?
   - Ⓐ basketball, handball, and baseball
   - Ⓑ basketball, tennis, and archery
   - Ⓒ basketball, tennis, and fencing

3. What is *Paralympics* short for?
   - Ⓐ Paralyzed Olympics
   - Ⓑ Parallel Olympics
   - Ⓒ Comparable Olympics

4. How many countries had athletes in the 2004 Summer Paralympics?
   - Ⓐ less than 23
   - Ⓑ more than 400
   - Ⓒ more than 136

Read the question, and write your answer.

What kinds of sports are played in the Summer Paralympics? What kinds of sports are played in the Winter Paralympics? _____

_____

_____

Chapter Quiz

Name _____ Date _____

Inspiring Excellence
Chapter 2, "Jean the Machine"

Number the events in order from 1 to 5.

____ A wheelchair-racing coach thought Jean Driscoll could become a top wheelchair racer.

____ Driscoll started playing wheelchair soccer and other wheelchair sports.

____ Driscoll could walk and ride a bike wearing special leg braces.

____ Driscoll fell off her bike and had to use a wheelchair.

____ Driscoll trained so hard she got the nickname Jean the Machine.

Number the events in order from 6 to 10.

____ Driscoll came in second in her first marathon.

____ Driscoll's coach talked her into doing the Chicago Marathon.

____ Driscoll helped send two athletes from Ghana to the Paralympics.

____ Driscoll won the 1990 Boston Marathon and broke the world record.

____ Driscoll trained for the Boston Marathon by pointing her chair into strong winds.

Read the question, and write your answer.

Why didn't Driscoll want to race in the Chicago Marathon? _____
_____
_____

Overcoming Adversity • Book 2

Chapter Quiz

Name _____ Date _____

Inspiring Excellence
Chapter 3, "The Will to Win"

Mark each statement *T* for true or *F* for false.

____ 1. Sarah Will started skiing when she was in college.

____ 2. Will's brother gave her a book on skiing for disabled people.

____ 3. After her accident, Will learned how to ski on a monoski.

____ 4. Will enjoyed monoskiing the very first time she tried it.

____ 5. Will won two silver medals in the 1992 Paralympics.

____ 6. Will can race down mountains at up to 60 miles per hour.

____ 7. Will wasn't able to attend the Canadian National Championships in 1992.

____ 8. Today, Will helps other disabled people discover adaptive sports.

____ 9. Will only helps disabled children learn to monoski.

____ 10. Will wants to get a team of monoskiers to do an exhibition at the X Games.

Read the question, and write your answer.

What are outriggers and how do they help monoskiers? _____

_____

_____

Chapter Quiz

Name _____ Date _____

Inspiring Excellence
Chapter 4, "Clearing the Bar"

Number the events in order from 1 to 5.

___ A family from Utah adopted Marlon Shirley.

___ Shirley won the high-jump event at a track meet for disabled athletes.

___ Shirley played football, basketball, and softball at school.

___ Bryan Hoddle watched Shirley in the high-jump event.

___ Shirley's left foot had to be amputated after a lawn mower ran over it.

Number the events in order from 6 to 10.

___ Many called Shirley "the fastest amputee in the world."

___ Shirley began training with athletes who are not disabled.

___ Shirley moved to Olympia, Washington.

___ Shirley won a silver medal in the 200-meter sprint at the Paralympics in Athens, Greece.

___ Shirley won the 100-meter sprint at the Paralympics in Sydney, Australia.

Read the question, and write your answer.

After what animal is Shirley's artificial foot named? Why is this a good name for Shirley's artificial foot? _____

_____

_____

Overcoming Adversity • Book 2

Chapter Quiz

Name _____ Date _____

Inspiring Excellence
Chapter 5, "A Bicycle Built for Two"

Fill in the bubble beside the answer for each question.

1. How much can Karissa Whitsell still see?
   - Ⓐ She can not see at all.
   - Ⓑ She can see just fine.
   - Ⓒ She can still see out of the corners of her eyes.

2. Why didn't Whitsell want to go to the tandem bicycle workshop for blind people when she first heard about it?
   - Ⓐ She thought she was "too cool," and she didn't think of herself as blind.
   - Ⓑ She was frightened to ride a bicycle because of her limited ability to see.
   - Ⓒ She didn't want to ride a bicycle with someone she didn't know.

3. What are mashers?
   - Ⓐ riders who like to ride in the higher gears
   - Ⓑ riders who win nearly every race
   - Ⓒ riders who sit on a tandem bicycle's back seat

4. What does Whitsell's partner Bob Westman do for her?
   - Ⓐ Westman acts as the pilot. He steers and stops their bicycle.
   - Ⓑ Westman rides behind Whitsell, telling her if traffic gets too close and warning her about potholes and trash on the road.
   - Ⓒ Westman acts as the stoker and pedals hard.

Read the question, and write your answer.

How do you think Whitsell feels about being able to ride a bicycle even though she is almost blind? _____

Overcoming Adversity • Book 2

Chapter Quiz

Name _____ Date _____

Inspiring Excellence
Chapter 6, "The Boy with Eight Legs"

Mark each statement *T* for true or *F* for false.

_____ 1. Rudy Garcia-Tolson went through 15 surgeries by the time he was five.

_____ 2. The doctors gave Garcia-Tolson a choice to use a wheelchair or have his legs amputated.

_____ 3. Garcia-Tolson decided to use a wheelchair.

_____ 4. Garcia-Tolson told his mother he would compete in the 2000 Paralympics.

_____ 5. By the time he was eight, Garcia-Tolson had won ten swimming medals.

_____ 6. Robin Williams and Scott Tinley did a triathlon with Garcia-Tolson.

_____ 7. Garcia-Tolson was a speaker and torch runner at the opening of the 2002 Winter Olympics.

_____ 8. Garcia-Tolson uses only one pair of artificial legs.

_____ 9. Garcia-Tolson sometimes tells kids an alligator bit off his legs.

_____ 10. Garcia-Tolson won a bronze medal in the 200-meter medley in 2004.

Read the question, and write your answer.

How many artificial legs does Garcia-Tolson have? Why do you think he has them? _____

_____

_____

Overcoming Adversity • Book 2

Thinking and Writing

Name _____ Date _____

Inspiring Excellence
Think About It

Write about or give an oral presentation for each question.

1. Why do you think the soldiers at Stoke Mandeville Hospital who played sports did better than those who did not play sports?

2. How are the Olympics and the Paralympics the same? How are they different?

3. Several of the athletes in this book played on their high school teams. Would a disabled athlete, such as Shirley, be welcomed on your school teams? Which teams?

Write About It

Choose one of the questions below. Write your answer on a sheet of paper.

1. Pretend you are Dr. Guttman. You are keeping a medical journal about one of your paralyzed patients who has decided to play in the Stoke Mandeville Games. Write two journal entries. One should be written before the patient starts to play and one after the Stoke Mandeville Games. Include details about your patient's health before and after the games. How does the patient feel about playing a sport?

2. Write a letter to one of the athletes in this book telling them how the story of their success has inspired you. Maybe you already play a sport and could ask one of these athletes for advice. You could also ask how you can encourage a disabled friend to take up a sport.

3. Complete the Cause and Effect Chart for this book.

Fluency Passages

Inspiring Excellence

Chapter 1 *pages 10 and 11*

*Driscoll began training hard. She used a special racing wheelchair	10
with two large tires in back and a smaller tire in front. The wheelchair was	25
sleek and fast. It was much lighter than everyday wheelchairs.	35
To move the wheelchair forward, she pushed the back wheels with	46
her hands. She had to wear special padded gloves to keep her hands from	60
getting cut and blistered.	64
Sometimes Driscoll would go as many as 150 miles a week to get	77
used to going long distances. Her arms needed to be very strong to power	91
the wheelchair, so she lifted weights. She worked so hard she got the	104
nickname Jean the Machine.	108
Driscoll's coach thought she should do the 1989 Chicago Marathon.	118
A marathon is a race that is 26.2 miles long. Driscoll didn't* want to do it.	134

Chapter 6 *page 43*

Garcia-Tolson was named Challenged Athlete of the Year in 2001.	10
He was also one of the speakers and torch runners at the opening of the	25
2002 Winter Olympics in Salt Lake City, Utah. He was only 13 at the time.	40
One of the things that helps him be such a great all-around athlete are	54
his legs—all eight of them! He has one pair for walking, one pair for	69
biking, and one pair for running. Of course, he counts his "stumps"—his	82
own legs without the artificial legs attached—as the fourth pair.	93
Garcia-Tolson is a spokesperson for the Challenged Athletes	101
Foundation. He goes to schools to talk to children about disabilities.	112
Sometimes when children see his stumps or artificial legs they ask him	124
what happened to his legs. He* doesn't mind their questions.	134

- The target rate for **Overcoming Adversity** is 130 wcpm. The asterisks (*) mark 130 words.
- Listen to the student read the passage. Count the number of words read in one minute and the number of errors.
- For the reading rate, subtract the number of errors from the total number of words read.
- Have students enter their scores on their **Fluency Graph.** See page 9.

Overcoming Adversity • Book 2

Answer Key

Building Background
Name _____ Date _____

Inspiring Excellence
What You Know
Write answers to these questions.

1. What are the Olympics? Who takes part in the Olympics? Do you know any events that are similar to the Olympics? **The Olympics are the world's largest sporting event. They are held once every four years. Athletes from all over the world participate in different events.**

2. What are some types of equipment that might help someone who cannot walk play a sport? **Ideas: special wheelchairs, scooters, leg braces, crutches**

3. What does *persistence* mean? What does *excellence* mean? Do you think you can have excellence without persistence? Why or why not? **Persistence is not giving up when things get tough. Excellence means the quality of being outstanding or extremely good. Answers will vary.**

Word Meanings
Matching
Look for these words as you read your chapter book. When you find a word, draw a line to connect the word with the correct definition.

amputation — a competition in which the competitors are not restricted to a certain way of performing
artificial — a birth defect in which part of the spinal cord and its coverings are exposed through a gap in the backbone
bilateral — an operation to remove an arm or leg from the body
freestyle — a group of two or more arranged one behind the other
spina bifida — having or involving two sides or parties
tandem — made by a human being, not by nature

24   Overcoming Adversity • Book 2

Inspiring Excellence

Chapter Quiz
Name _____ Date _____

Inspiring Excellence
Chapter 1, "The First Paralympics"
Fill in the bubble beside the answer for each question.

1. Who were the athletes in the first Stoke Mandeville Games?
   - ● soldiers who had injured their spinal cords in World War II
   - Ⓑ doctors and nurses at the Stoke Mandeville Hospital in England
   - Ⓒ good friends of Dr. Ludwig Guttman

2. What sports did athletes play at the first Stoke Mandeville Games?
   - Ⓐ basketball, handball, and baseball
   - ● basketball, tennis, and archery
   - Ⓒ basketball, tennis, and fencing

3. What is *Paralympics* short for?
   - Ⓐ Paralyzed Olympics
   - ● Parallel Olympics
   - Ⓒ Comparable Olympics

4. How many countries had athletes in the 2004 Summer Paralympics?
   - Ⓐ less than 23
   - Ⓑ more than 400
   - ● more than 136

Read the question, and write your answer.

What kinds of sports are played in the Summer Paralympics? What kinds of sports are played in the Winter Paralympics? **Summer Paralympic sports include track, cycling, soccer, sailing, swimming, basketball, tennis and fencing; some Winter Paralympic sports are downhill skiing, cross-country skiing, and hockey.**

26   Overcoming Adversity • Book 2

Inspiring Excellence

Chapter Quiz
Name _____ Date _____

Inspiring Excellence
Chapter 2, "Jean the Machine"
Number the events in order from 1 to 5.

- **4** A wheelchair-racing coach thought Jean Driscoll could become a top wheelchair racer.
- **3** Driscoll started playing wheelchair soccer and other wheelchair sports.
- **1** Driscoll could walk and ride a bike wearing special leg braces.
- **2** Driscoll fell off her bike and had to use a wheelchair.
- **5** Driscoll trained so hard she got the nickname Jean the Machine.

Number the events in order from 6 to 10.

- **7** Driscoll came in second in her first marathon.
- **6** Driscoll's coach talked her into doing the Chicago Marathon.
- **10** Driscoll helped send two athletes from Ghana to the Paralympics.
- **9** Driscoll won the 1990 Boston Marathon and broke the world record.
- **8** Driscoll trained for the Boston Marathon by pointing her chair into strong winds.

Read the question, and write your answer.

Why didn't Driscoll want to race in the Chicago Marathon? **A marathon is 26.2 miles long; Driscoll thought that was too long and that she wouldn't be able to complete the course.**

Overcoming Adversity • Book 2   27

Inspiring Excellence

Chapter Quiz
Name _____ Date _____

Inspiring Excellence
Chapter 3, "The Will to Win"
Mark each statement *T* for true or *F* for false.

- **F** 1. Sarah Will started skiing when she was in college.
- **T** 2. Will's brother gave her a book on skiing for disabled people.
- **T** 3. After her accident, Will learned how to ski on a monoski.
- **F** 4. Will enjoyed monoskiing the very first time she tried it.
- **F** 5. Will won two silver medals in the 1992 Paralympics.
- **T** 6. Will can race down mountains at up to 60 miles per hour.
- **F** 7. Will wasn't able to attend the Canadian National Championships in 1992.
- **T** 8. Today, Will helps other disabled people discover adaptive sports.
- **F** 9. Will only helps disabled children learn to monoski.
- **T** 10. Will wants to get a team of monoskiers to do an exhibition at the X Games.

Read the question, and write your answer.

What are outriggers and how do they help monoskiers? **Outriggers are poles that have small skis on them; they help monoskiers stay upright and turn as they ski down a mountain.**

28   Overcoming Adversity • Book 2

Inspiring Excellence

Answer Key

Chapter Quiz

Name _____ Date _____

Inspiring Excellence
Chapter 4, "Clearing the Bar"

Number the events in order from 1 to 5.

__2__ A family from Utah adopted Marlon Shirley.
__5__ Shirley won the high-jump event at a track meet for disabled athletes.
__3__ Shirley played football, basketball, and softball at school.
__4__ Bryan Hoddle watched Shirley in the high-jump event.
__1__ Shirley's left foot had to be amputated after a lawn mower ran over it.

Number the events in order from 6 to 10.

__8__ Many called Shirley "the fastest amputee in the world."
__10__ Shirley began training with athletes who are not disabled.
__6__ Shirley moved to Olympia, Washington.
__9__ Shirley won a silver medal in the 200-meter sprint at the Paralympics in Athens, Greece.
__7__ Shirley won the 100-meter sprint at the Paralympics in Sydney, Australia.

Read the question, and write your answer.

After what animal is Shirley's artificial foot named? Why is this a good name for Shirley's artificial foot? **Shirley's artificial foot is called "the Cheetah." The cheetah is the fastest animal on land, and like the cheetah, Shirley runs fast.**

Overcoming Adversity • Book 2 — 29

Inspiring Excellence

Chapter Quiz

Name _____ Date _____

Inspiring Excellence
Chapter 5, "A Bicycle Built for Two"

Fill in the bubble beside the answer for each question.

1. How much can Karissa Whitsell still see?
   - Ⓐ She can not see at all.
   - Ⓑ She can see just fine.
   - ● She can still see out of the corners of her eyes.

2. Why didn't Whitsell want to go to the tandem bicycle workshop for blind people when she first heard about it?
   - ● She thought she was "too cool," and she didn't think of herself as blind.
   - Ⓑ She was frightened to ride a bicycle because of her limited ability to see.
   - Ⓒ She didn't want to ride a bicycle with someone she didn't know.

3. What are mashers?
   - ● riders who like to ride in the higher gears
   - Ⓑ riders who win nearly every race
   - Ⓒ riders who sit on a tandem bicycle's back seat

4. What does Whitsell's partner Bob Westman do for her?
   - Ⓐ Westman acts as the pilot. He steers and stops their bicycle.
   - ● Westman rides behind Whitsell, telling her if traffic gets too close and warning her about potholes and trash on the road.
   - Ⓒ Westman acts as the stoker and pedals hard.

Read the question, and write your answer.

How do you think Whitsell feels about being able to ride a bicycle even though she is almost blind? **Ideas: excited; happy; lucky because being able to see is an important part of riding a bicycle**

30 — *Overcoming Adversity • Book 2*

Inspiring Excellence

Chapter Quiz

Name _____ Date _____

Inspiring Excellence
Chapter 6, "The Boy with Eight Legs"

Mark each statement T for true or F for false.

__T__ 1. Rudy Garcia-Tolson went through 15 surgeries by the time he was five.
__T__ 2. The doctors gave Garcia-Tolson a choice to use a wheelchair or have his legs amputated.
__F__ 3. Garcia-Tolson decided to use a wheelchair.
__F__ 4. Garcia-Tolson told his mother he would compete in the 2000 Paralympics.
__F__ 5. By the time he was eight, Garcia-Tolson had won ten swimming medals.
__T__ 6. Robin Williams and Scott Tinley did a triathlon with Garcia-Tolson.
__T__ 7. Garcia-Tolson was a speaker and torch runner at the opening of the 2002 Winter Olympics.
__F__ 8. Garcia-Tolson uses only one pair of artificial legs.
__T__ 9. Garcia-Tolson sometimes tells kids an alligator bit off his legs.
__F__ 10. Garcia-Tolson won a bronze medal in the 200-meter medley in 2004.

Read the question, and write your answer.

How many artificial legs does Garcia-Tolson have? Why do you think he has them? **six; each pair is different and made to fit the specific sport or activity he uses it for**

Overcoming Adversity • Book 2 — 31

Inspiring Excellence

Thinking and Writing

Name _____ Date _____

Inspiring Excellence
Think About It

Write about or give an oral presentation for each question.

1. Why do you think the soldiers at Stoke Mandeville Hospital who played sports did better than those who did not play sports?
   Ideas: Physical activity and exercise are a very important part of one's health. Paralyzed people can still exercise the parts of their bodies that are not paralyzed. Exercise helps give people a better outlook on life.

2. How are the Olympics and the Paralympics the same? How are they different? **Ideas: same: both are big sporting events held every four years, some sports are the same; both give gold, silver, and bronze medals; athletes come from many different countries to compete; different: the Olympics are bigger than the Paralympics; the athletes in the Paralympics all have a physical disability.**

3. Several of the athletes in this book played on their high school teams. Would a disabled athlete, such as Shirley, be welcomed on your school teams? Which teams? **Answers will vary.**

Write About It

Choose one of the questions below. Write your answer on a sheet of paper.

1. Pretend you are Dr. Guttman. You are keeping a medical journal about one of your paralyzed patients who has decided to play in the Stoke Mandeville Games. Write two journal entries. One should be written before the patient starts to play and one after the Stoke Mandeville Games. Include details about your patient's health before and after the games. How does the patient feel about playing a sport?

2. Write a letter to one of the athletes in this book telling them how the story of their success has inspired you. Maybe you already play a sport and could ask one of these athletes for advice. You could also ask how you can encourage a disabled friend to take up a sport.

3. Complete the Cause and Effect Chart for this book.

32 — *Overcoming Adversity • Book 2*

Inspiring Excellence

Overcoming Adversity • Book 2 — 35

Building Background

Name _____ Date _____

Playing through Pain
What You Know

Write answers to these questions.

1. Who is your favorite athlete? Describe him or her. Include the person's actions both on and off the field. _____

2. What is a role model? How should a role model act? How does someone become a role model? _____

3. On a map, locate Puerto Rico and Nicaragua and the cities Montreal and Pittsburgh. Calculate the distance between Puerto Rico and Nicaragua, Puerto Rico and Montreal, and Puerto Rico and Pittsburgh.

_____

_____

4. Begin the What I Know/What I Learned Chart for this book. Complete the What I Know portion.

Word Meanings
Definitions

Look for these words as you read your chapter book. When you find one of these words, write its definition.

contract: _____

draft: _____

javelin: _____

mourn: _____

respect: _____

survivors: _____

Word Lists

Playing through Pain

	Unfamiliar Words	Word Meanings	Proper Nouns
Chapter 1	announcer donated radio		New York Pittsburgh Pirates Puerto Rico Roberto Clemente
Chapter 2	bought business college finally honest importance muscles practicing taught though value	javelin respect	Carolina Olympics Spanish
Chapter 3	bonus promised talent uniform	contract draft	Brooklyn Dodgers English French Montreal United States
Chapter 4	athlete autographs competition despite headaches hero honor injury malaria stadium surgery television terrible		Gold Glove Most Valuable Player National League World Series
Chapter 5	artificial citizens deaf expensive extra furniture notice special		Nicaragua Vera Christina Zabala Pennsylvania
Chapter 6	acre earthquake equipment flown prepare relief soccer statue usually	mourn survivors	Baseball Hall of Fame Christmas

Overcoming Adversity • Book 3

37

Chapter Quiz

Name _____ Date _____

Playing through Pain
Chapter 1, "Born to Play"

Mark each statement *T* for true or *F* for false.

_____ 1. Roberto Clemente said he was born to fly planes.

_____ 2. As a boy, Clemente sometimes used a tin can as a baseball.

_____ 3. By the time he was 19, Clemente was in the major leagues.

_____ 4. Clemente played for the Pittsburgh Pirates.

_____ 5. Clemente hit mostly to right field.

_____ 6. Clemente was known for his fast pitch.

_____ 7. Clemente is considered one of the greatest baseball players ever.

_____ 8. Clemente wasn't a very nice person.

_____ 9. Clemente was ashamed of his Puerto Rican roots.

_____ 10. Clemente's parents taught him right from wrong.

Read the question, and write your answer.

How do you think Clemente's childhood affected his views toward racism and toward his own heritage? _____

_____

_____

Chapter Quiz

Name _____ Date _____

Playing through Pain
Chapter 2, "Baseball Kid"

Fill in the bubble beside the answer for each question.

1. What language did Clemente's family speak?
   - Ⓐ French
   - Ⓑ English
   - Ⓒ Spanish

2. Where did Clemente's father work?
   - Ⓐ in a baseball team office
   - Ⓑ in the sugarcane fields
   - Ⓒ in a grocery store

3. How did Clemente earn money to pay for a bike?
   - Ⓐ delivering newspapers
   - Ⓑ delivering milk
   - Ⓒ picking up pennies

4. What did Clemente learn from his job?
   - Ⓐ Hard work feels good.
   - Ⓑ Work is no fun.
   - Ⓒ It is easy to make money.

Read the question, and write your answer.

Did Clemente follow his parents' plan for his career? Explain your answer.

_____

_____

Overcoming Adversity • Book 3

Chapter Quiz

Name _____ Date _____

Playing through Pain
Chapter 3, "A Dream Come True"

Number the events in order from 1 to 5.

____ Clemente wanted to quit because he never got to play.

____ Clemente made 40 dollars a week playing baseball in the winter leagues.

____ Clemente began playing on a baseball team.

____ A softball coach saw Clemente hit tin cans.

____ At age 14, Clemente made the softball team.

Number the events in order from 6 to 10.

____ Clemente signed a contract to play for the Brooklyn Dodgers.

____ Major league scouts came to Puerto Rico looking for new players.

____ The Pittsburgh Pirates drafted Clemente.

____ The Dodgers tried to hide Clemente.

____ Clemente played in the minor leagues in Montreal.

Read the question, and write your answer.

Why is this chapter called "A Dream Come True"? Explain your answer.

_____

_____

_____

Chapter Quiz

Name _____ Date _____

Playing through Pain
Chapter 4, "Baseball Hero"

Fill in the bubble beside the answer for each question.

1. How long did Clemente play for the Pirates?
   - Ⓐ 1 year
   - Ⓑ 8 years
   - Ⓒ 18 years

2. How did Clemente treat the fans?
   - Ⓐ He played catch with them.
   - Ⓑ He was rude to them.
   - Ⓒ He spent time talking with them.

3. What did Clemente do when he was not named Most Valuable Player?
   - Ⓐ threw his bat
   - Ⓑ worked harder
   - Ⓒ blamed the coach

4. Why do people remember Clemente's last hit in 1972?
   - Ⓐ It was a grand slam.
   - Ⓑ It was his 3,000th hit.
   - Ⓒ It won the World Series.

Read the question, and write your answer.

How did Clemente become a baseball hero? What problems did he face?

_____

_____

_____

Overcoming Adversity • Book 3

Chapter Quiz

Name _____ Date _____

Playing through Pain
Chapter 5, "Off-Field Hero"

Mark each statement *T* for true or *F* for false.

____ 1. Every winter Clemente went to Hawaii.

____ 2. Clemente met his wife in Puerto Rico.

____ 3. Clemente and his wife had three girls.

____ 4. Clemente taught children to play baseball.

____ 5. Clemente told children to be good citizens.

____ 6. Clemente did not like being a role model for children.

____ 7. Not many people came to Roberto Clemente Night at Three Rivers Stadium.

____ 8. Clemente was proud to be Latino.

____ 9. A salesman thought Clemente was poor because he was Latino.

____ 10. Clemente liked to talk about the good things he did.

Read the question, and write your answer.

Why might people say that Clemente was a humble hero? _____

_____

_____

Chapter Quiz

Name _____ Date _____

Playing through Pain
Chapter 6, "Last Season"

Number the events in order from 1 to 5.

____ An earthquake hit Nicaragua.

____ Clemente heard that supplies were not getting to the people who needed them.

____ Clemente wanted to work on plans for a new sports center.

____ Clemente collected food and clothes to help earthquake victims.

____ After the baseball season, Clemente went home to Puerto Rico.

Number the events in order from 6 to 10.

____ To honor Clemente's dream, people gave money to build Sports City.

____ Clemente decided to take the supplies to Nicaragua himself.

____ On New Year's Eve, the plane crashed.

____ Clemente became the first Latino voted into the National Baseball Hall of Fame.

____ The relief plane was too heavy when it took off.

Read the question, and write your answer.

What led to Clemente's death, and how have people honored his life?

_____

_____

_____

Overcoming Adversity • Book 3   43

Thinking and Writing

Name _____ Date _____

Playing through Pain
Think About It

Write about or give an oral presentation for each question.

1. If Clemente had not died on the plane, what do you think he would be doing today? _____

2. Give examples from the book to explain the title *Playing through Pain*.
   _____
   _____

3. What are some lessons Clemente learned from his parents?
   _____
   _____

4. Clemente's nickname was The Great One. What would yours be? Why?
   _____
   _____

Write About It

Choose one of the questions below. Write your answer on a sheet of paper.

1. Make a trading card about yourself. Draw your picture. Write about things you have done.

2. You are a role model for younger children. What advice would you give them?

3. It is Roberto Clemente Day at your school. You will give a speech about Clemente's life. Tell why people remember him.

4. Complete the What I Know/What I Learned Chart for this book.

Fluency Passages

Playing through Pain

Chapter 1 *page 2*

*He could hit to any part of the field. He would dive for balls and	15
catch pop flies. He raced around the bases at lightning speed.	26
But most of all, Clemente was known for his strong right arm. One	39
radio sports announcer said Clemente could catch the baseball in one state	51
and throw out the runner in another state.	59
Fame came to Clemente late in his life. He won many awards. He	72
became known as one of the greatest baseball players ever. He was much	85
more than a great baseball player, however. He was also a great person.	98
Clemente was proud of his roots in Puerto Rico. He welcomed young	110
Latino players to his team. He donated his time and money to help those	124
from his homeland who were in* need.	131

Chapter 4 *page 22*

*But the fans liked the way Clemente played. They loved to watch	12
him leap to catch the ball. They loved to see him throw the ball while he	28
was still in the air. He did not think twice about crashing against a wall or	44
diving into the grass to make a catch. He could bat well too.	57
Clemente was happy to spend hours signing autographs. He would	67
always take time to talk to fans. Clemente's team began to get better. At	81
the same time, he was playing better. By the end of his second season he	96
was batting .311.	99
Even though his baseball career was going well, there were some other	111
problems in Clemente's life. While he was on a trip home, a drunk driver	125
ran through a red light.* The driver's car crashed into Clemente's car.	137

- The target rate for **Overcoming Adversity** is 130 wcpm. The asterisks (*) mark 130 words.
- Listen to the student read the passage. Count the number of words read in one minute and the number of errors.
- For the reading rate, subtract the number of errors from the total number of words read.
- Have students enter their scores on their **Fluency Graph.** See page 9.

Overcoming Adversity • Book 3

Answer Key

Building Background

Name _____ Date _____

Playing through Pain
What You Know
Write answers to these questions.

1. Who is your favorite athlete? Describe him or her. Include the person's actions both on and off the field. **Answers will vary.**
2. What is a role model? How should a role model act? How does someone become a role model? **Accept reasonable responses.**
3. On a map, locate Puerto Rico and Nicaragua and the cities Montreal and Pittsburgh. Calculate the distance between Puerto Rico and Nicaragua, Puerto Rico and Montreal, and Puerto Rico and Pittsburgh. **Puerto Rico and Nicaragua: about 1400 miles; Puerto Rico and Montreal: about 1900 miles; Puerto Rico and Pittsburgh: about 1700 miles**
4. Begin the What I Know/What I Learned Chart for this book. Complete the What I Know portion.

Word Meanings
Definitions
Look for these words as you read your chapter book. When you find one of these words, write its definition.

contract: **a legally binding agreement**
draft: **to pick people for a special purpose, such as for a sports team**
javelin: **a thin shaft thrown for distance in track-and-field events; a light spear**
mourn: **to feel or show sorrow or grief when someone dies**
respect: **high regard**
survivors: **those who remain alive**

36 — Overcoming Adversity • Book 3
Playing through Pain

Chapter Quiz

Name _____ Date _____

Playing through Pain
Chapter 1, "Born to Play"
Mark each statement *T* for true or *F* for false.

F 1. Roberto Clemente said he was born to fly planes.
T 2. As a boy, Clemente sometimes used a tin can as a baseball.
T 3. By the time he was 19, Clemente was in the major leagues.
T 4. Clemente played for the Pittsburgh Pirates.
F 5. Clemente hit mostly to right field.
F 6. Clemente was known for his fast pitch.
T 7. Clemente is considered one of the greatest baseball players ever.
F 8. Clemente wasn't a very nice person.
F 9. Clemente was ashamed of his Puerto Rican roots.
T 10. Clemente's parents taught him right from wrong.

Read the question, and write your answer.

How do you think Clemente's childhood affected his views toward racism and toward his own heritage? **Ideas: grew up respecting all people; no hate or racism in his home; was proud to be Latino; proud of his Puerto Rican roots**

38 — Overcoming Adversity • Book 3
Playing through Pain

Chapter Quiz

Name _____ Date _____

Playing through Pain
Chapter 2, "Baseball Kid"
Fill in the bubble beside the answer for each question.

1. What language did Clemente's family speak?
   Ⓐ French
   Ⓑ English
   ● Spanish

2. Where did Clemente's father work?
   Ⓐ in a baseball team office
   ● in the sugarcane fields
   Ⓒ in a grocery store

3. How did Clemente earn money to pay for a bike?
   Ⓐ delivering newspapers
   ● delivering milk
   Ⓒ picking up pennies

4. What did Clemente learn from his job?
   ● Hard work feels good.
   Ⓑ Work is no fun.
   Ⓒ It is easy to make money.

Read the question, and write your answer.

Did Clemente follow his parents' plan for his career? Explain your answer. **His parents wanted him to go to college and become an engineer; his conduct on and off the field reflected their values and wishes.**

Overcoming Adversity • Book 3 — 39
Playing through Pain

Chapter Quiz

Name _____ Date _____

Playing through Pain
Chapter 3, "A Dream Come True"
Number the events in order from 1 to 5.

5 Clemente wanted to quit because he never got to play.
4 Clemente made 40 dollars a week playing baseball in the winter leagues.
3 Clemente began playing on a baseball team.
1 A softball coach saw Clemente hit tin cans.
2 At age 14, Clemente made the softball team.

Number the events in order from 6 to 10.

7 Clemente signed a contract to play for the Brooklyn Dodgers.
6 Major league scouts came to Puerto Rico looking for new players.
10 The Pittsburgh Pirates drafted Clemente.
9 The Dodgers tried to hide Clemente.
8 Clemente played in the minor leagues in Montreal.

Read the question, and write your answer.

Why is this chapter called "A Dream Come True"? Explain your answer. **Clemente's dream, to play on a major league baseball team in the United States, came true for him.**

40 — Overcoming Adversity • Book 3
Playing through Pain

---

46 — Overcoming Adversity • Book 3

Answer Key

Chapter Quiz

Name _____ Date _____

Playing through Pain
Chapter 4, "Baseball Hero"
Fill in the bubble beside the answer for each question.

1. How long did Clemente play for the Pirates?
   - Ⓐ 1 year
   - Ⓑ 8 years
   - ● 18 years

2. How did Clemente treat the fans?
   - Ⓐ He played catch with them.
   - Ⓑ He was rude to them.
   - ● He spent time talking with them.

3. What did Clemente do when he was not named Most Valuable Player?
   - Ⓐ threw his bat
   - ● worked harder
   - Ⓒ blamed the coach

4. Why do people remember Clemente's last hit in 1972?
   - Ⓐ It was a grand slam.
   - ● It was his 3,000th hit.
   - Ⓒ It won the World Series.

Read the question, and write your answer.

How did Clemente become a baseball hero? What problems did he face?
Ideas: hard work, outstanding player, kind to fans, played through pain, named Most Valuable Player in the World Series; racism, people made fun of his English, physical injuries, malaria

Overcoming Adversity • Book 3   41

Chapter Quiz

Name _____ Date _____

Playing through Pain
Chapter 5, "Off-Field Hero"
Mark each statement *T* for true or *F* for false.

- **F** 1. Every winter Clemente went to Hawaii.
- **T** 2. Clemente met his wife in Puerto Rico.
- **F** 3. Clemente and his wife had three girls.
- **T** 4. Clemente taught children to play baseball.
- **T** 5. Clemente told children to be good citizens.
- **F** 6. Clemente did not like being a role model for children.
- **F** 7. Not many people came to Roberto Clemente Night at Three Rivers Stadium.
- **T** 8. Clemente was proud to be Latino.
- **T** 9. A salesman thought Clemente was poor because he was Latino.
- **F** 10. Clemente liked to talk about the good things he did.

Read the question, and write your answer.

Why might people say that Clemente was a humble hero? **Ideas: worked to help people and to make the world a better place; did not boast or brag about his accomplishments and deeds**

42   Overcoming Adversity • Book 3

Chapter Quiz

Name _____ Date _____

Playing through Pain
Chapter 6, "Last Season"
Number the events in order from 1 to 5.

- **3** An earthquake hit Nicaragua.
- **5** Clemente heard that supplies were not getting to the people who needed them.
- **2** Clemente wanted to work on plans for a new sports center.
- **4** Clemente collected food and clothes to help earthquake victims.
- **1** After the baseball season, Clemente went home to Puerto Rico.

Number the events in order from 6 to 10.

- **9** To honor Clemente's dream, people gave money to build Sports City.
- **6** Clemente decided to take the supplies to Nicaragua himself.
- **8** On New Year's Eve, the plane crashed.
- **10** Clemente became the first Latino voted into the National Baseball Hall of Fame.
- **7** The relief plane was too heavy when it took off.

Read the question, and write your answer.

What led to Clemente's death, and how have people honored his life?
Ideas: died while helping provide supplies after an earthquake in Nicaragua, was on an overloaded plane that crashed; Sports City completed, U.S. schools and a coliseum in Puerto Rico named after him, Roberto Clemente Award

Overcoming Adversity • Book 3   43

Thinking and Writing

Name _____ Date _____

Playing through Pain
Think About It
Write about or give an oral presentation for each question.

1. If Clemente had not died on the plane, what do you think he would be doing today? **Answers will vary.**

2. Give examples from the book to explain the title *Playing through Pain*.
Ideas: Clemente suffered from physical problems, injuries, and emotional distress; people made fun of his accent and his English.

3. What are some lessons Clemente learned from his parents?
Ideas: to work hard; to be good, honest, and kind; to respect others; not to hate

4. Clemente's nickname was The Great One. What would yours be? Why?
Answers will vary.

Write About It
Choose one of the questions below. Write your answer on a sheet of paper.

1. Make a trading card about yourself. Draw your picture. Write about things you have done.

2. You are a role model for younger children. What advice would you give them?

3. It is Roberto Clemente Day at your school. You will give a speech about Clemente's life. Tell why people remember him.

4. Complete the What I Know/What I Learned Chart for this book.

44   Overcoming Adversity • Book 3

Overcoming Adversity • Book 3   47

Building Background

Name _____ Date _____

Once There Were Two
What You Know

Write answers to these questions.

1. Find out more about the beginnings of baseball in the United States. How did it start? When were the first major leagues organized? Where were the teams located? Write your answers on a separate piece of paper.

2. What is segregation? How did it affect the lives of African Americans, especially those who lived in the South? _____

3. How do civil rights laws protect the rights of all people?

4. Who are your favorite baseball stars? Why do you like them?

Word Meanings
Matching

Look for these words as you read your chapter book. When you find a word, draw a line to connect the word with the correct definition.

integrate   ethically, behave in a way that is honest and good

league   separation of groups, usually based on race

morally   to end segregation, to open to people of all races

prejudice   exaggerated story, one that is hard to believe

segregation   association of groups or people united for a common purpose

tall tale   dislike or mistreatment of a person or group because of their race, religion, or country of origin

48   Overcoming Adversity • Book 4

Word Lists

Once There Were Two

Chapter	Proper Nouns	Word Meanings	Unfamiliar Words
Chapter 1	Babe Ruth, Griffith Stadium, James "Cool Papa" Bell, Jimmie Crutchfield, Josh Gibson, Leroy "Satchel" Paige, National League, New York Yankees, Oscar Charleston, Pittsburgh Crawfords, Washington, D.C., William Julius "Judy" Johnson	league, segregation	famous, favorite, heroes, muscular, separate, special
Chapter 2	Adrian Constantine, Brooklyn, "Chief Tokahoma", Confederate, George Stovey, Jackie Robinson, Knickerbockers, Moses Fleetwood "Fleet" Walker, National Association of Baseball Players, New Jersey, Philadelphia, Union	prejudice	accidentally, continued, guards, influence, injured, recruit
Chapter 3	Great Depression, Michigan, U.S. Supreme Court		businesses, challenges, character, developed, professional, restaurants, stomachs, theaters, though
Chapter 4	Arkansas, Cuban Stars, Detroit Stars, Kansas City Monarchs, Martín Dihigo, Mexico, Rube Foster, St. Louis Giants	tall tale	determined, expressive, hesitation, interviews, positions, schedules
Chapter 5	Babe Didrickson, Branch Rickey, Jay "Dizzy" Dean, J. L. Wilkinson, Jesse Owens, Newark Eagles, Puerto Rico, Spanish, Venezuela		capable, climate, competitions, ghost, guests, philosophy, regular, usually
Chapter 6	Brooklyn Dodgers, Charlie Thomas, Don Newcombe, Roy Campanella	integrate, morally	barrier, haunted, humiliation, promised, situation

Overcoming Adversity • Book 4

Chapter Quiz

Name _____ Date _____

Once There Were Two
Chapter 1, "Unknown Sports Heroes"

Mark each statement *T* for true or *F* for false.

_____ 1. The American League record for home runs was 84.

_____ 2. Babe Ruth hit 60 home runs to set the American League record.

_____ 3. Ruth's home run record beat Josh Gibson's record.

_____ 4. Ruth was called "the white Josh Gibson."

_____ 5. Gibson played in the Negro Leagues.

_____ 6. Many experts say the best baseball team ever was the 1936 Pittsburgh Crawfords.

_____ 7. Leroy "Satchel" Paige is considered one of the greatest pitchers of all time.

_____ 8. Starting in 1920, African American ballplayers played in the major leagues.

_____ 9. African American players did not want to play in the major leagues.

_____ 10. Caucasian fans did not go to Negro League games.

Read the question, and write your answer.

Why is the title of this chapter "Unknown Sports Heroes"?

_____

_____

_____

Chapter Quiz

Name _____ Date _____

Once There Were Two
Chapter 2, "Play Ball!"

Fill in the bubble beside the answer for each question.

1. Where do some people believe the first baseball game was played?
   - Ⓐ California
   - Ⓑ New Jersey
   - Ⓒ Ohio

2. What helped spread the game of baseball throughout the country?
   - Ⓐ newspapers
   - Ⓑ radio
   - Ⓒ the U.S. Civil War

3. Which coach refused to allow his Caucasian players to play against teams with African American players?
   - Ⓐ "Fleet" Walker
   - Ⓑ Babe Ruth
   - Ⓒ Cap Anson

4. Who was the first African American player in the major leagues?
   - Ⓐ Moses Fleetwood "Fleet" Walker
   - Ⓑ Leroy "Satchel" Paige
   - Ⓒ Josh Gibson

Read the question, and write your answer.

Explain the irony of the role of the U.S. Civil War in the spread of baseball.

_____

_____

Overcoming Adversity • Book 4

Chapter Quiz

Name _____ Date _____

Once There Were Two
Chapter 3, "Building Communities"

Fill in the bubble beside the answer for each question.

1. What did "Jim Crow" laws do?
   - Ⓐ gave everyone the same rights
   - Ⓑ took away the rights of African Americans
   - Ⓒ let cities start baseball teams

2. What did the Supreme Court rule in 1896?
   - Ⓐ It was legal to keep African Americans "separate but equal."
   - Ⓑ Anyone could play baseball.
   - Ⓒ both A and B

3. Where did the first all-black professional team start?
   - Ⓐ Atlanta, Georgia
   - Ⓑ New York City
   - Ⓒ Los Angeles, California

4. Why did the Page Fence Giants sleep on the train?
   - Ⓐ They could not stay in most hotels because they were African American.
   - Ⓑ They could get to the games faster.
   - Ⓒ They were tired from playing baseball and needed to sleep right away.

Read the question, and write your answer.

What challenges did African American baseball teams face? Why were these teams important to African American culture? _____

_____

_____

Chapter Quiz

Name _____ Date _____

Once There Were Two
Chapter 4, "A Roster of Greats"

Mark each statement *T* for true or *F* for false.

____ 1. James "Cool Papa" Bell was the fastest man in baseball.

____ 2. Bell could beat his own ball to second base.

____ 3. Gibson had the highest lifetime batting average in the Negro Leagues.

____ 4. Martín Dihigo could play all nine positions and won three home run crowns.

____ 5. Dihigo is in the Baseball Hall of Fame in three countries.

____ 6. Paige was too busy being funny to be a good pitcher.

____ 7. The "father of black baseball" is Rube Foster of the Chicago Giants.

____ 8. Foster and seven others formed the Negro National League.

____ 9. The first NNL teams were in the South.

____ 10. Each state had just one Negro League team.

Read the question, and write your answer.

What do you think happened to the Negro National League? Explain your answer. _____

_____

_____

_____

Overcoming Adversity • Book 4

Chapter Quiz

Name _____ Date _____

Once There Were Two
Chapter 5, "Equals on the Field"

Fill in the bubble beside the answer for each question.

1. African American and Caucasian teams played each other in "barnstorming" games, which were
    - Ⓐ games played in another country.
    - Ⓑ traveling games played all over the United States.
    - Ⓒ games played without the usual rules.

2. Why did Caucasian all-star teams play against African American teams?
    - Ⓐ to help end segregation
    - Ⓑ for easy wins
    - Ⓒ to make money in the off-season

3. Which teams won most of those games?
    - Ⓐ Caucasian teams won 80 percent of the time.
    - Ⓑ African American teams won 60 percent of the time.
    - Ⓒ They each won an equal number.

4. What did the Negro Leagues do to bring in fans?
    - Ⓐ They rigged lights and played at night.
    - Ⓑ They played blindfolded, invented "ghost ball," and had special guests.
    - Ⓒ both A and B

Read the question, and write your answer.

How did African American baseball players manage to make a living?

_____

_____

Chapter Quiz

Name _____ Date _____

Once There Were Two
Chapter 6, "A Beginning and an End"

Mark each statement *T* for true or *F* for false.

_____ 1. Branch Rickey felt segregation was right.

_____ 2. Some people threatened Jackie Robinson's life.

_____ 3. Paige never got the chance to play in the major leagues.

_____ 4. After African Americans started to play on major league teams, the Negro Leagues still drew large crowds.

_____ 5. The Negro Leagues played an important part in baseball history.

_____ 6. The Negro Leagues are still in existence.

_____ 7. Rickey became general manager of the Brooklyn Dodgers in 1942.

_____ 8. Even though he was very talented, Robinson was never named the league's most valuable player.

_____ 9. Despite taunting, Robinson never lost his temper on the field.

Read the question, and write your answer.

Explain how the story of the Negro Leagues relates to the theme **Overcoming Adversity.** _____

_____

_____

_____

Overcoming Adversity • Book 4   55

Thinking and Writing

Name _____ Date _____

Once There Were Two
Think About It

Write about or give an oral presentation for each question.

1. What other areas of society had "barriers"? Are all the "barriers" gone?
   _____
   _____

2. How did segregation hurt the major leagues? _____
   _____

3. Why did Rickey fight to get an African American player on his team?
   _____
   _____

Write About It

Choose one of the questions below. Write your answer on a sheet of paper.

1. Make up a sports "hall of fame" with players of all genders and races.

2. Find out more about one of the players named in the book. Write a report on that player.

3. Learn more about Robinson. Then write about how it might have felt to be the first African American player to break the color barrier.

4. Complete the Content Web for this book.

Fluency Passages

Once There Were Two

Chapter 1 *page 2*

*His right sleeve was rolled above his muscular forearm. The brim of	12
his cap was pushed back. His large body looked relaxed.	22
But the fans weren't fooled. They could read the look on his face. It	36
sent them a clear message: "I'm going to do it again."	47
"It" was hitting a home run. The fans wished for it as much as the	62
man did. *Whack!* They got their wish sooner than they expected.	73
The batter hit the first pitch high toward center field. It cleared the	86
fence and sailed right out of the park. The fans went wild. They yelled.	100
They jumped. They hugged. Some threw their hats in the air.	111
Any home run would be cause for joy. But this one was special. It	125
was the 84th home run* the man had hit that season.	136

Chapter 6 *page 44*

*Paige was the exception. He was about 40 years old in 1948 when	13
Cleveland signed him. He pitched his last major league game in 1965. He	26
was around 57 years old!	31
Major league teams had the cash to bring the best African American	43
players to the major leagues. Fans wanted to watch the top players. The	56
Negro Leagues could not afford the top players, so fewer and fewer fans	69
came to their games. When they started, the Negro Leagues gave African	81
American players a place to play baseball. After the players were accepted	93
in the major leagues, the Negro Leagues folded.	101
The Negro Leagues were an important part of baseball history. They	112
showed that African American players were as good as Caucasian players	123
and that they deserved to play in* the same league.	133

- The target rate for **Overcoming Adversity** is 130 wcpm. The asterisks (*) mark 130 words.
- Listen to the student read the passage. Count the number of words read in one minute and the number of errors.
- For the reading rate, subtract the number of errors from the total number of words read.
- Have students enter their scores on their **Fluency Graph.** See page 9.

Overcoming Adversity • Book 4

Answer Key

Building Background

Name _____ Date _____

Once There Were Two
What You Know

Write answers to these questions.

1. Find out more about the beginnings of baseball in the United States. How did it start? When were the first major leagues organized? Where were the teams located? Write your answers on a separate piece of paper.
   Accept reasonable responses.
2. What is segregation? How did it affect the lives of African Americans, especially those who lived in the South? **separation of people based on skin color; led to segregated facilities and strict laws separating people of different races**
3. How do civil rights laws protect the rights of all people? **provide equal opportunities and fair treatment for all, especially in voting, employment, and education**
4. Who are your favorite baseball stars? Why do you like them?
   Answers will vary.

Word Meanings
Matching

Look for these words as you read your chapter book. When you find a word, draw a line to connect the word with the correct definition.

integrate — ethically, behave in a way that is honest and good
league — separation of groups, usually based on race
morally — to end segregation, to open to people of all races
prejudice — exaggerated story, one that is hard to believe
segregation — association of groups or people united for a common purpose
tall tale — dislike or mistreatment of a person or group because of their race, religion, or country of origin

48 — Overcoming Adversity • Book 4

Once There Were Two

Chapter Quiz

Name _____ Date _____

Once There Were Two
Chapter 1, "Unknown Sports Heroes"

Mark each statement *T* for true or *F* for false.

F 1. The American League record for home runs was 84.
T 2. Babe Ruth hit 60 home runs to set the American League record.
F 3. Ruth's home run record beat Josh Gibson's record.
F 4. Ruth was called "the white Josh Gibson."
T 5. Gibson played in the Negro Leagues.
T 6. Many experts say the best baseball team ever was the 1936 Pittsburgh Crawfords.
T 7. Leroy "Satchel" Paige is considered one of the greatest pitchers of all time.
F 8. Starting in 1920, African American ballplayers played in the major leagues.
F 9. African American players did not want to play in the major leagues.
F 10. Caucasian fans did not go to Negro League games.

Read the question, and write your answer.

Why is the title of this chapter "Unknown Sports Heroes"?
It is about famous African American baseball players who have been forgotten but who paved the way toward integration.

50 — Overcoming Adversity • Book 4

Once There Were Two

Chapter Quiz

Name _____ Date _____

Once There Were Two
Chapter 2, "Play Ball!"

Fill in the bubble beside the answer for each question.

1. Where do some people believe the first baseball game was played?
   Ⓐ California
   ● New Jersey
   Ⓒ Ohio
2. What helped spread the game of baseball throughout the country?
   Ⓐ newspapers
   Ⓑ radio
   ● the U.S. Civil War
3. Which coach refused to allow his Caucasian players to play against teams with African American players?
   Ⓐ "Fleet" Walker
   Ⓑ Babe Ruth
   ● Cap Anson
4. Who was the first African American player in the major leagues?
   ● Moses Fleetwood "Fleet" Walker
   Ⓑ Leroy "Satchel" Paige
   Ⓒ Josh Gibson

Read the question, and write your answer.

Explain the irony of the role of the U.S. Civil War in the spread of baseball.
Enslaved African Americans were freed during the Civil War, but even though they were free, discrimination prevented them from playing on Caucasian teams.

Overcoming Adversity • Book 4 — 51

Once There Were Two

Chapter Quiz

Name _____ Date _____

Once There Were Two
Chapter 3, "Building Communities"

Fill in the bubble beside the answer for each question.

1. What did "Jim Crow" laws do?
   Ⓐ gave everyone the same rights
   ● took away the rights of African Americans
   Ⓒ let cities start baseball teams
2. What did the Supreme Court rule in 1896?
   ● It was legal to keep African Americans "separate but equal."
   Ⓑ Anyone could play baseball.
   Ⓒ both A and B
3. Where did the first all-black professional team start?
   Ⓐ Atlanta, Georgia
   ● New York City
   Ⓒ Los Angeles, California
4. Why did the Page Fence Giants sleep on the train?
   ● They could not stay in most hotels because they were African American.
   Ⓑ They could get to the games faster.
   Ⓒ They were tired from playing baseball and needed to sleep right away.

Read the question, and write your answer.

What challenges did African American baseball teams face? Why were these teams important to African American culture? **Ideas: players could not stay in hotels or eat in restaurants, strict segregation in the South; players served as role models, provided jobs, entertainment, were successful African American-owned businesses**

52 — Overcoming Adversity • Book 4

Once There Were Two

---

58 — Overcoming Adversity • Book 4

Answer Key

Chapter Quiz

Name _____ Date _____

Once There Were Two
Chapter 4, "A Roster of Greats"
Mark each statement *T* for true or *F* for false.

- **T** 1. James "Cool Papa" Bell was the fastest man in baseball.
- **F** 2. Bell could beat his own ball to second base.
- **T** 3. Gibson had the highest lifetime batting average in the Negro Leagues.
- **T** 4. Martín Dihigo could play all nine positions and won three home run crowns.
- **T** 5. Dihigo is in the Baseball Hall of Fame in three countries.
- **F** 6. Paige was too busy being funny to be a good pitcher.
- **T** 7. The "father of black baseball" is Rube Foster of the Chicago Giants.
- **T** 8. Foster and seven others formed the Negro National League.
- **F** 9. The first NNL teams were in the South.
- **F** 10. Each state had just one Negro League team.

Read the question, and write your answer.

What do you think happened to the Negro National League? Explain your answer. **It declined as African Americans begin to play for integrated major league teams.**

Overcoming Adversity • Book 4   53

Once There Were Two

Chapter Quiz

Name _____ Date _____

Once There Were Two
Chapter 5, "Equals on the Field"
Fill in the bubble beside the answer for each question.

1. African American and Caucasian teams played each other in "barnstorming" games, which were
   - Ⓐ games played in another country.
   - ● traveling games played all over the United States.
   - Ⓒ games played without the usual rules.

2. Why did Caucasian all-star teams play against African American teams?
   - Ⓐ to help end segregation
   - Ⓑ for easy wins
   - ● to make money in the off-season

3. Which teams won most of those games?
   - Ⓐ Caucasian teams won 80 percent of the time.
   - ● African American teams won 60 percent of the time.
   - Ⓒ They each won an equal number.

4. What did the Negro Leagues do to bring in fans?
   - Ⓐ They rigged lights and played at night.
   - Ⓑ They played blindfolded, invented "ghost ball," and had special guests.
   - ● both A and B

Read the question, and write your answer.

How did African American baseball players manage to make a living? **played year-round; played in countries south of U.S. border**

54   Overcoming Adversity • Book 4

Once There Were Two

Chapter Quiz

Name _____ Date _____

Once There Were Two
Chapter 6, "A Beginning and an End"
Mark each statement *T* for true or *F* for false.

- **F** 1. Branch Rickey felt segregation was right.
- **T** 2. Some people threatened Jackie Robinson's life.
- **F** 3. Paige never got the chance to play in the major leagues.
- **F** 4. After African Americans started to play on major league teams, the Negro Leagues still drew large crowds.
- **T** 5. The Negro Leagues played an important part in baseball history.
- **F** 6. The Negro Leagues are still in existence.
- **T** 7. Rickey became general manager of the Brooklyn Dodgers in 1942.
- **F** 8. Even though he was very talented, Robinson was never named the league's most valuable player.
- **T** 9. Despite taunting, Robinson never lost his temper on the field.

Read the question, and write your answer.

Explain how the story of the Negro Leagues relates to the theme Overcoming Adversity. **Ideas: African Americans continued to play baseball and developed their own leagues in spite of segregation, poor pay, and challenges. The players also helped integrate sports.**

Overcoming Adversity • Book 4   55

Once There Were Two

Thinking and Writing

Name _____ Date _____

Once There Were Two
Think About It
Write about or give an oral presentation for each question.

1. What other areas of society had "barriers"? Are all the "barriers" gone? **Ideas: business, sports, education, military, astronaut training. Probably not, because people still have prejudices.**

2. How did segregation hurt the major leagues? **Idea: They missed out on many good players, loyal fans, and money.**

3. Why did Rickey fight to get an African American player on his team? **Ideas: He saw how segregation hurt people; he knew African American players would be good for baseball.**

Write About It
Choose one of the questions below. Write your answer on a sheet of paper.

1. Make up a sports "hall of fame" with players of all genders and races.
2. Find out more about one of the players named in the book. Write a report on that player.
3. Learn more about Robinson. Then write about how it might have felt to be the first African American player to break the color barrier.
4. Complete the Content Web for this book.

56   Overcoming Adversity • Book 4

Once There Were Two

Overcoming Adversity • Book 4   59

Building Background

Name _____ Date _____

Walls of Water
What You Know

Write answers to these questions.

1. What are some of the different kinds of warnings that the government issues? _____
_____

2. Do you think people should be forced to obey government warnings and evacuation orders? Explain your answer. _____

3. Where are floods most likely to occur? _____
_____

4. What purposes do dams serve? _____
_____

5. What is the American Red Cross? What are its goals? _____
_____

Word Meanings
Synonyms

Look for these words as you read your chapter book. When you find a word, write a synonym for the word.

debris: _____

disaster: _____

levee: _____

tragedy: _____

tsunami: _____

victims: _____

Word Lists

Walls of Water

Unfamiliar Words	Word Meanings	Proper Nouns	
able, boulders, collapsed, destroyed, flood, ruins, survivor	debris, disaster	Johnstown, Pennsylvania, Stony Creek River	Chapter 1
build, clothing, relatives, rescue	tragedy, victims	American Red Cross, Children's Aid Society, Clara Barton	Chapter 2
area, attracted, businesses, channel, property, route, worse		Cambria Iron Company, Conemaugh River	Chapter 3
effect, operate, system, thousand	levee	Gulf of Mexico, Minnesota, Mississippi River Basin, National Weather Service	Chapter 4
acres, effort, recovered		National Guard, Ohio Valley	Chapter 5
example, predicting, type	tsunami	Belgium, England, Hawaii, Netherlands	Chapter 6

Overcoming Adversity • Book 5

Chapter Quiz

Name _____ Date _____

Walls of Water
Chapter 1, "The Johnstown Flood, 1889"

Number the events in order from 1 to 5.

___ Tons of lumber rolled down the river.

___ It rained for days in the spring of 1889.

___ Store owners moved their goods to high shelves.

___ A man on horseback shouted a warning to the townspeople.

___ A small dam on the river broke.

Number the events in order from 6 to 10.

___ The flood piled debris 40 feet high at the railroad bridge.

___ A wall of water more than 35 feet high crashed into the valley.

___ When the rush of water was over, survivors were stranded in the rubble.

___ Soon after the warning, the South Fork Dam gave way.

___ The pile of debris caught fire.

Read the question, and write your answer.

Why did so many people die during the 1889 Johnstown flood?

_____

_____

_____

Chapter Quiz

Name _____ Date _____

Walls of Water
Chapter 2, "Rescue and Relief"

Mark each statement *T* for true or *F* for false.

____ 1. The people of Johnstown cleaned up the flood without help.

____ 2. The Red Cross had handled many major disasters before the Johnstown flood.

____ 3. Clara Barton said the Red Cross would not help the people of Johnstown.

____ 4. The flood victims needed food, shelter, and clothing.

____ 5. More than 50 children were left without parents.

____ 6. The stories told by flood survivors were full of tragedy and luck.

____ 7. One man floated in the floodwaters for 17 hours.

____ 8. People on a roof watched helplessly as others floated by.

____ 9. One man was flung out of his house and into his office.

____ 10. The floodwaters kept people away from the fire at the bridge.

Read the question, and write your answer.

Why did some people face more of a danger during the flood?

_____

_____

_____

Chapter Quiz

Name _____ Date _____

Walls of Water
Chapter 3, "A Look Back at Johnstown"

Fill in the bubble beside the answer for each question.

1. Where is Johnstown located?
   - Ⓐ on Lake Superior
   - Ⓑ near the fork of three rivers
   - Ⓒ on the coast of the Atlantic Ocean

2. Why was the South Fork Dam built?
   - Ⓐ to irrigate crops in the nearby farms
   - Ⓑ to keep boats off the river
   - Ⓒ to make a lake to feed water to the canal

3. What did slag from the steel mills do?
   - Ⓐ filled in the river channels and made the water move faster
   - Ⓑ made good farmland along the river
   - Ⓒ washed downstream from Johnstown

4. Who owned the land around the lake?
   - Ⓐ mill workers
   - Ⓑ the South Fork Fishing and Hunting Club
   - Ⓒ both A and B

Read the question, and write your answer.

Describe Johnstown and its citizens before the flood. _____

_____

_____

Chapter Quiz

Name _____ Date _____

Walls of Water
Chapter 4, "The Great Flood of 1993"

Mark each statement *T* for true or *F* for false.

____ 1. The Mississippi River runs from Minnesota to the Gulf of Mexico.

____ 2. People have built locks, dams, and canals to keep the river from overflowing.

____ 3. People who live along the river get used to flooding now and then.

____ 4. The melting of winter snow has little to do with spring flooding.

____ 5. There was no flood warning for the people who lived along the river.

Number the events in order from 1 to 5.

____ Water ran off the land into rivers, raising the water levels.

____ A dam broke, and the Great Flood of 1993 began.

____ Heavy snow fell in the winter, and spring rains melted the snow.

____ When a big storm hit in June 1993, people got ready for a flood.

____ The rain started in the fall of 1992, and the ground filled with water.

Read the question, and write your answer.

What factors led to the Great Flood of 1993? Why was it far more costly than the Johnstown flood? _____

_____

_____

_____

Overcoming Adversity • Book 5   65

Chapter Quiz

Name _____ Date _____

Walls of Water
Chapter 5, "After the Flood"

Mark each statement *T* for true or *F* for false.

_____ 1. In 1993, record rains fell in nine states.

_____ 2. City officials in the Mississippi River Basin were unprepared.

_____ 3. All the relief workers were unable to save lives, homes, or businesses.

_____ 4. Help came from all parts of the country.

_____ 5. More people died in the Great Flood of 1993 than in the Johnstown Flood of 1889.

_____ 6. Flood victims' immediate needs are food, drinking water, and medical care.

_____ 7. Government help is not given to flood victims after natural disasters.

_____ 8. National Guard troops give support after major floods.

_____ 9. Service groups find temporary shelter for the flood victims.

Read the question, and write your answer.

Why is it important for government officials and relief agencies to work together after a natural disaster? _____

_____

_____

Chapter Quiz

Name _____ Date _____

Walls of Water
Chapter 6, "What Causes Floods?"

Fill in the bubble beside the answer for each question.

1. A sudden rush of swirling water is called
   - Ⓐ a runoff.
   - Ⓑ a flash flood.
   - Ⓒ a 100-year flood.

2. Why does flooding cause more damage now than in previous times?
   - Ⓐ Rivers were wider and could take more water.
   - Ⓑ There were fewer people and businesses located in floodplains then.
   - Ⓒ both A and B

3. What is another name for a tidal wave caused by underwater earthquakes?
   - Ⓐ a tsunami
   - Ⓑ a floodplain
   - Ⓒ a 500-year flood

4. What rules have some states made to keep people safe from floods?
   - Ⓐ Homes may not be rebuilt in flood zones.
   - Ⓑ Wetlands must be kept dry.
   - Ⓒ both A and B

Read the question, and write your answer.

What steps can cities take to avoid devastating floods? _____

_____

Overcoming Adversity • Book 5

Thinking and Writing

Name _____ Date _____

Walls of Water
Think About It

Write about or give an oral presentation for each question.

1. How did steel mills make the Johnstown flood worse? _____
   _____

2. *Foreshadowing* is hinting at what will take place later in the story. Give an example of foreshadowing in the Johnstown flood chapters.
   _____
   _____

3. Why do you think so many people help flood victims and other strangers in need? _____
   _____

4. Why are wetlands important? _____
   _____

Write About It

Choose one of the questions below. Write your answer on a sheet of paper.

1. The Red Cross helped the people of Johnstown. Write a report on how the Red Cross started and what the Red Cross does today.

2. Pretend you are a survivor of the Johnstown Flood. Write a story about what happened to you and your family.

3. Complete the Compare and Contrast Diagram for this book.

Fluency Passages

Walls of Water

Chapter 1 *pages 2 and 3*

*It kept raining. It rained all morning, and the water rose. Store	12
owners moved their goods to high shelves. At noon a small dam broke on	26
the Stony Creek River. The dam had been holding back logs. When it	39
broke, tons of lumber went rolling down the river.	48
Many people stood by the banks of the river. They watched as the	61
logs tumbled through town. Still, the people of Johnstown did not worry.	73
They were used to flooding now and then.	81
It kept raining. The water rose higher. Some people left their jobs at	94
noon. They went home to check on their families. A flood might keep the	108
families indoors. They would need drinking water and food. It might take a	121
few days for the storm to pass.	128
"Roll up* those rugs!"	132
"Empty that cabinet!"	135

Chapter 6 *pages 38 and 39*

*Flooding is caused by lots of water that has nowhere to go. The	13
water can come from rain. Storms blow in from the ocean. They pour over	27
mountains. They drift across the land.	33
The water can also come from snow. A string of warm days will send	47
melted snow shooting down mountains.	52
No matter where it comes from, the water has to go someplace. Some	65
of the water from rain and snow soaks into the ground. The rest runs off.	80
Runoff is greater where the land is steep. Water trickles down slick rock	93
faces and ice caps. It forms little creeks. The creeks flow into streams. The	107
streams flow into rivers. The rivers flow into bigger rivers. The water flows	120
down the rivers and into the sea.	127
About 200 years* ago, rivers were wider.	134

- The target rate for **Overcoming Adversity** is 130 wcpm. The asterisks (*) mark 130 words.
- Listen to the student read the passage. Count the number of words read in one minute and the number of errors.
- For the reading rate, subtract the number of errors from the total number of words read.
- Have students enter their scores on their **Fluency Graph.** See page 9.

Overcoming Adversity • Book 5

Answer Key

Building Background

Name _____ Date _____

Walls of Water
What You Know
Write answers to these questions.

1. What are some of the different kinds of warnings that the government issues? **Ideas: consumer label warnings; weather warnings on radio or television; house-to-house evacuation orders**

2. Do you think people should be forced to obey government warnings and evacuation orders? Explain your answer. **Accept reasonable responses.**

3. Where are floods most likely to occur? **along rivers and in low-lying coastal regions**

4. What purposes do dams serve? **Ideas: control flow of water; conserve water; protect lowlands from flooding**

5. What is the American Red Cross? What are its goals? **organization that helps people during emergencies; provides medical care, supplies, shelter**

Word Meanings
Synonyms
Look for these words as you read your chapter book. When you find a word, write a synonym for the word.

debris: **trash, junk, rubbish**
disaster: **catastrophe, calamity**
levee: **bank, dam**
tragedy: **disaster, misfortune**
tsunami: **tidal wave**
victims: **fatalities**

Chapter Quiz

Name _____ Date _____

Walls of Water
Chapter 1, "The Johnstown Flood, 1889"
Number the events in order from 1 to 5.

4 Tons of lumber rolled down the river.
1 It rained for days in the spring of 1889.
2 Store owners moved their goods to high shelves.
5 A man on horseback shouted a warning to the townspeople.
3 A small dam on the river broke.

Number the events in order from 6 to 10.

8 The flood piled debris 40 feet high at the railroad bridge.
7 A wall of water more than 35 feet high crashed into the valley.
10 When the rush of water was over, survivors were stranded in the rubble.
6 Soon after the warning, the South Fork Dam gave way.
9 The pile of debris caught fire.

Read the question, and write your answer.

Why did so many people die during the 1889 Johnstown flood?
Ideas: did not believe danger was real; did not heed warnings

Chapter Quiz

Name _____ Date _____

Walls of Water
Chapter 2, "Rescue and Relief"
Mark each statement *T* for true or *F* for false.

F 1. The people of Johnstown cleaned up the flood without help.
F 2. The Red Cross had handled many major disasters before the Johnstown flood.
F 3. Clara Barton said the Red Cross would not help the people of Johnstown.
T 4. The flood victims needed food, shelter, and clothing.
T 5. More than 50 children were left without parents.
T 6. The stories told by flood survivors were full of tragedy and luck.
T 7. One man floated in the floodwaters for 17 hours.
F 8. People on a roof watched helplessly as others floated by.
T 9. One man was flung out of his house and into his office.
F 10. The floodwaters kept people away from the fire at the bridge.

Read the question, and write your answer.

Why did some people face more of a danger during the flood?
Victims in the water floated into the bridge fire.

Chapter Quiz

Name _____ Date _____

Walls of Water
Chapter 3, "A Look Back at Johnstown"
Fill in the bubble beside the answer for each question.

1. Where is Johnstown located?
   Ⓐ on Lake Superior
   ● near the fork of three rivers
   Ⓒ on the coast of the Atlantic Ocean

2. Why was the South Fork Dam built?
   Ⓐ to irrigate crops in the nearby farms
   Ⓑ to keep boats off the river
   ● to make a lake to feed water to the canal

3. What did slag from the steel mills do?
   ● filled in the river channels and made the water move faster
   Ⓑ made good farmland along the river
   Ⓒ washed downstream from Johnstown

4. Who owned the land around the lake?
   Ⓐ mill workers
   ● the South Fork Fishing and Hunting Club
   Ⓒ both A and B

Read the question, and write your answer.

Describe Johnstown and its citizens before the flood. **strong city of 10,000; had stores, schools, churches, and steel mills; many people worked in the steel mills**

70   Overcoming Adversity • Book 5

# Answer Key

Chapter Quiz

Name _____ Date _____

Walls of Water
Chapter 4, "The Great Flood of 1993"

Mark each statement *T* for true or *F* for false.

- **T** 1. The Mississippi River runs from Minnesota to the Gulf of Mexico.
- **T** 2. People have built locks, dams, and canals to keep the river from overflowing.
- **T** 3. People who live along the river get used to flooding now and then.
- **F** 4. The melting of winter snow has little to do with spring flooding.
- **F** 5. There was no flood warning for the people who lived along the river.

Number the events in order from 1 to 5.

- **3** Water ran off the land into rivers, raising the water levels.
- **5** A dam broke, and the Great Flood of 1993 began.
- **2** Heavy snow fell in the winter, and spring rains melted the snow.
- **4** When a big storm hit in June 1993, people got ready for a flood.
- **1** The rain started in the fall of 1992, and the ground filled with water.

Read the question, and write your answer.

What factors led to the Great Flood of 1993? Why was it far more costly than the Johnstown flood? **Ideas: a rainy fall, followed by wettest summer in 98 years, no place for water to go, dam burst; Great Flood affected a much wider region and many more people, whole towns were destroyed**

Chapter Quiz

Name _____ Date _____

Walls of Water
Chapter 5, "After the Flood"

Mark each statement *T* for true or *F* for false.

- **T** 1. In 1993, record rains fell in nine states.
- **F** 2. City officials in the Mississippi River Basin were unprepared.
- **F** 3. All the relief workers were unable to save lives, homes, or businesses.
- **T** 4. Help came from all parts of the country.
- **F** 5. More people died in the Great Flood of 1993 than in the Johnstown Flood of 1889.
- **T** 6. Flood victims' immediate needs are food, drinking water, and medical care.
- **F** 7. Government help is not given to flood victims after natural disasters.
- **T** 8. National Guard troops give support after major floods.
- **T** 9. Service groups find temporary shelter for the flood victims.

Read the question, and write your answer.

Why is it important for government officials and relief agencies to work together after a natural disaster? **Big and very different kinds of problems arise during natural disasters; coordination is needed.**

Chapter Quiz

Name _____ Date _____

Walls of Water
Chapter 6, "What Causes Floods?"

Fill in the bubble beside the answer for each question.

1. A sudden rush of swirling water is called
   - Ⓐ a runoff.
   - ● a flash flood.
   - Ⓒ a 100-year flood.

2. Why does flooding cause more damage now than in previous times?
   - Ⓐ Rivers were wider and could take more water.
   - Ⓑ There were fewer people and businesses located in floodplains then.
   - ● both A and B

3. What is another name for a tidal wave caused by underwater earthquakes?
   - ● a tsunami
   - Ⓑ a floodplain
   - Ⓒ a 500-year flood

4. What rules have some states made to keep people safe from floods?
   - ● Homes may not be rebuilt in flood zones.
   - Ⓑ Wetlands must be kept dry.
   - Ⓒ both A and B

Read the question, and write your answer.

What steps can cities take to avoid devastating floods? **limit development and develop open parkland along rivers; develop/maintain wetlands; develop warning systems**

Thinking and Writing

Name _____ Date _____

Walls of Water
Think About It

Write about or give an oral presentation for each question.

1. How did steel mills make the Johnstown flood worse? **Slag from the mills narrowed the river channels and made the water move faster.**

2. *Foreshadowing* is hinting at what will take place later in the story. Give an example of foreshadowing in the Johnstown flood chapters. **Ideas: The South Fork Dam leaked; another dam broke; water was rising.**

3. Why do you think so many people help flood victims and other strangers in need? **Ideas: People realize they might need help in the future; people have skills that are needed.**

4. Why are wetlands important? **Ideas: Wetlands soak up lots of water; they help keep water from moving on and flooding towns.**

Write About It

Choose one of the questions below. Write your answer on a sheet of paper.

1. The Red Cross helped the people of Johnstown. Write a report on how the Red Cross started and what the Red Cross does today.

2. Pretend you are a survivor of the Johnstown Flood. Write a story about what happened to you and your family.

3. Complete the Compare and Contrast Diagram for this book.

Overcoming Adversity • Book 5   71

Building Background

Name _____ Date _____

Robinson Crusoe
What You Know

Write answers to these questions.

1. What can happen to a ship during a storm? _____
   _____

2. How do you think sailing 300 years ago differed from sailing today?
   _____
   _____

3. What kinds of skills would you need to survive on a desert island?
   _____
   _____

4. If you were stranded on a desert island, what kind of person would you like to have with you? _____
   _____

Word Meanings
Definitions

Look for these words as you read your chapter book. When you find one of these words, write its definition.

canoe: _____

capture: _____

desperate: _____

profit: _____

shelter: _____

spyglass: _____

72   Overcoming Adversity • Book 6

Word Lists

Robinson Crusoe

Unfamiliar Words	Word Meanings	Proper Nouns	
bought, business, hurricane, merchant, miracle, pirate, plantation, promise, signal, situation, sugarcane, worse	profit	Africa, Brazil, England, London, Robinson Crusoe, Xury, Yarmouth, York	Chapter 1
canvas, dozen, explored, flattened, hammock, routine, strength	shelter, spyglass		Chapter 2
busy, convinced, loyal, taught	canoe	Friday	Chapter 3
	desperate		Chapter 4
	shipwrecked		Chapter 4
captives, confused, married, passenger, prisoners			Chapter 5
constantly, famous, fiction, leather, raise, successful, valuable	capture	Alexander Selkirk, *Cinque ports*, Daniel Defoe, Juan Fernández, Scotland, William Dampier, Woodes Rodgers, *Weymouth*	Chapter 6

Overcoming Adversity • Book 6

Chapter Quiz

Name _____ Date _____

Robinson Crusoe
Chapter 1, "Going to Sea"

Number the events in order from 1 to 5.

____ During a storm Robinson Crusoe gets seasick and promises never to sail again.

____ Crusoe wants to become a sailor, but his family tries to talk him out of it.

____ A nearby ship sends a rowboat to the rescue.

____ Crusoe sails from London without telling his parents.

____ When a second storm hits, the ship begins to sink.

Number the events in order from 6 to 10.

____ On Crusoe's next trip pirates attack the ship and capture the crew.

____ The people in Yarmouth are kind to the shipwrecked sailors.

____ Pirates take Crusoe and the crew to a town in Africa and force them to work.

____ Crusoe sells African gold dust for a profit when he returns to England.

____ Crusoe sails to Africa and learns how to be a good sailor.

Read the question, and write your answer.

Why do you think Crusoe left home without telling his parents?

_____

_____

_____

Chapter Quiz

Name _____ Date _____

Robinson Crusoe
Chapter 2, "Stranded on an Island"

Mark each statement *T* for true or *F* for false.

___ 1. Crusoe's ship had washed out to sea.

___ 2. Crusoe was sad that everyone else had been lost.

___ 3. Crusoe was not able to bring supplies from the ship.

___ 4. One night the ship fell apart in a storm.

___ 5. Crusoe's stay on the island began in September 1659.

___ 6. Crusoe taught himself to build furniture and make useful things.

___ 7. Crusoe built a fence around his camp to keep people out.

___ 8. Crusoe liked to sleep late in the morning and hunt at midday.

___ 9. After Crusoe got sick, he was afraid to explore the rest of the island.

___ 10. Crusoe caught animals on the island.

Read the question, and write your answer.

What was Crusoe's daily schedule? _____

_____

_____

Overcoming Adversity • Book 6   75

Chapter Quiz

Name _____ Date _____

Robinson Crusoe
Chapter 3, "A Footprint in the Sand"

Number the events in order from 1 to 5.

____ Several years passed before Crusoe saw another footprint.

____ Crusoe used animal skins to make a hat.

____ Crusoe was alone on the island for 11 years.

____ Crusoe built a canoe.

____ One day Crusoe found a human footprint.

Number the events in order from 6 to 10.

____ Through his spyglass Crusoe saw men dancing around a fire.

____ Crusoe called the man "Friday" and taught him English.

____ The men had two captives, but one of the captives escaped from them.

____ Crusoe fired his gun in the air as the captive ran toward him.

____ Crusoe smiled and signaled for the man to come forward.

Read the question, and write your answer.

Why does Crusoe say that the year he found Friday was his happiest year on the island? _____

_____

_____

Chapter Quiz

Name _____ Date _____

Robinson Crusoe
Chapter 4, "Two Others Join Us"

Fill in the bubble beside the answer for each question.

1. After Crusoe learned about the strange men on Friday's island, what did he plan to do?
   - Ⓐ go to Friday's island
   - Ⓑ go see the men who were there
   - Ⓒ both A and B

2. What did Friday say they needed to get to the island?
   - Ⓐ a lot of food
   - Ⓑ a bigger boat
   - Ⓒ both A and B

3. What kept Friday and Crusoe from starting their trip?
   - Ⓐ wind
   - Ⓑ hot sun
   - Ⓒ rain

4. Why would the other men on the island stay away from now on?
   - Ⓐ They found other food.
   - Ⓑ They were afraid of the guns.
   - Ⓒ Their canoes were wrecked.

Read the question, and write your answer.

How did Crusoe and Friday celebrate when they found Friday's father and the Spaniard? _____

_____

_____

Overcoming Adversity • Book 6

77

Chapter Quiz

Name _____ Date _____

Robinson Crusoe
Chapter 5, "Rescued!"

Number the events in order from 1 to 5.

____ Using a spyglass, Crusoe saw an English ship sailing toward him.

____ The captain said Crusoe ruled the island.

____ Crusoe, Friday, the captain, and some sailors recaptured the ship.

____ Sailors brought three captives ashore.

____ When the sailors fell asleep, Friday and Crusoe set the captives free.

Number the events in order from 6 to 10.

____ Crusoe went back to Brazil.

____ Friday and Crusoe sailed to England.

____ In 1694 Crusoe visited the island.

____ Crusoe found out his plantation in Brazil had done well.

____ Friday stayed on the island when Crusoe left.

Read the question, and write your answer.

Why do you think Crusoe wanted to return to the island?

_____

_____

_____

Chapter Quiz

Name _____ Date _____

Robinson Crusoe
Chapter 6, "Was Crusoe Real?"

Fill in the bubble beside the answer for each question.

1. Who may have been the real Crusoe?
   - Ⓐ Daniel Defoe
   - Ⓑ Alexander Selkirk
   - Ⓒ William Dampier

2. A *privateer* is a person who
   - Ⓐ is hired to recapture enemy ships.
   - Ⓑ makes maps for the captain.
   - Ⓒ steers the ship.

3. Dampier and Selkirk ended up in the
   - Ⓐ Spice Islands.
   - Ⓑ Juan Fernández islands.
   - Ⓒ Hawaiian Islands.

4. Selkirk became pilot of the
   - Ⓐ *Weymouth*.
   - Ⓑ *Cinque Ports*.
   - Ⓒ *Duke*.

Read the question, and write your answer.

Do you think *Robinson Crusoe* is fiction or nonfiction? Explain your answer.

_____

_____

Overcoming Adversity • Book 6

Thinking and Writing

Name _____ Date _____

Robinson Crusoe
Think About It

Write about or give an oral presentation for each question.

1. How did Crusoe feel when he saw the footprint in the sand? Why?

2. What skills did Crusoe use to stay alive on the island?

3. Give some examples of foreshadowing from the story.

Write About It

Choose one of the questions below. Write your answer on a sheet of paper.

1. Crusoe was a survivor. What would you do to survive alone on an island? What would you do to keep from being bored?

2. Tell how this story fits the theme **Overcoming Adversity.** Give specific examples from the book.

3. Pretend you are Crusoe. Write a journal entry about one day on the island.

4. Complete the Book Report Form for this book.

Fluency Passages

Robinson Crusoe

Chapter 2 *pages 12 and 13*

*I was wet and cold. I had no clothes except the ones on my back, and	16
they were in bad shape. I had no food and no water. There was no shelter	32
from the weather.	35
It was getting dark, so I had to find freshwater fast. I was lucky to find	51
some nearby.	53
All I had was a knife and a small box. I was afraid that wild animals	69
might attack me that night, so I climbed a tree. I cut a piece of wood from	86
the tree to use as a tool if any animal attacked me. I was so tired that I	104
spent my first night on the island sleeping in the tree.	115
I awoke to sunshine and clear weather. From my place in the tree, I	129
could* see the ship.	133

Chapter 5 *page 35*

*It would be ten hours before the tide was high enough for their ship	14
to leave. I got a gun and went to find the captives.	26
Friday and I crept up on the three men, who had been tied up some	41
distance away. The men were surprised when I called out to them. One	54
man began to cry.	58
"Am I talking to a god or a man?" he asked.	69
I told him I was an Englishman. He appeared to be English also. He	83
said he was the captain of the ship. His men had turned against him and	98
had taken over his ship. They planned to kill him, his first mate, and a	113
passenger.	114
Lucky for the captain, his captors had wandered into the forest and	126
had fallen asleep before* they could carry out their plan.	136

- The target rate for **Overcoming Adversity** is 130 wcpm. The asterisks (*) mark 130 words.
- Listen to the student read the passage. Count the number of words read in one minute and the number of errors.
- For the reading rate, subtract the number of errors from the total number of words read.
- Have students enter their scores on their **Fluency Graph.** See page 9.

Answer Key

Building Background

Robinson Crusoe
What You Know
Write answers to these questions.

1. What can happen to a ship during a storm? **Ideas: shipwreck, sink, be blown off course**

2. How do you think sailing 300 years ago differed from sailing today? **Ideas: no modern technology, lack of navigational tools, no motors, no weather warnings, few good maps**

3. What kinds of skills would you need to survive on a desert island? **Ideas: how to build shelter, find food, make tools**

4. If you were stranded on a desert island, what kind of person would you like to have with you? **Ideas: resourceful person, someone who can build things, a problem solver**

Word Meanings
Definitions
Look for these words as you read your chapter book. When you find one of these words, write its definition.

canoe: **long, narrow, lightweight boat**
capture: **to catch and hold by force**
desperate: **hopeless, reckless**
profit: **the amount of money left after all expenses have been paid**
shelter: **a covering or something that protects someone from the weather**
spyglass: **a small, handheld telescope**

72 — Overcoming Adversity • Book 6 — *Robinson Crusoe*

Chapter Quiz

Robinson Crusoe
Chapter 1, "Going to Sea"
Number the events in order from 1 to 5.

3 During a storm Robinson Crusoe gets seasick and promises never to sail again.
1 Crusoe wants to become a sailor, but his family tries to talk him out of it.
5 A nearby ship sends a rowboat to the rescue.
2 Crusoe sails from London without telling his parents.
4 When a second storm hits, the ship begins to sink.

Number the events in order from 6 to 10.

9 On Crusoe's next trip pirates attack the ship and capture the crew.
6 The people in Yarmouth are kind to the shipwrecked sailors.
10 Pirates take Crusoe and the crew to a town in Africa and force them to work.
8 Crusoe sells African gold dust for a profit when he returns to England.
7 Crusoe sails to Africa and learns how to be a good sailor.

Read the question, and write your answer.

Why do you think Crusoe left home without telling his parents?
Ideas: knew they would disapprove; was an adult; did not think about parents worrying

74 — Overcoming Adversity • Book 6 — *Robinson Crusoe*

Chapter Quiz

Robinson Crusoe
Chapter 2, "Stranded on an Island"
Mark each statement *T* for true or *F* for false.

F 1. Crusoe's ship had washed out to sea.
T 2. Crusoe was sad that everyone else had been lost.
F 3. Crusoe was not able to bring supplies from the ship.
T 4. One night the ship fell apart in a storm.
T 5. Crusoe's stay on the island began in September 1659.
T 6. Crusoe taught himself to build furniture and make useful things.
F 7. Crusoe built a fence around his camp to keep people out.
F 8. Crusoe liked to sleep late in the morning and hunt at midday.
F 9. After Crusoe got sick, he was afraid to explore the rest of the island.
T 10. Crusoe caught animals on the island.

Read the question, and write your answer.

What was Crusoe's daily schedule? **in the morning hunt for animals, make tools; nap in afternoon; in the evening work on tools; wrote almost every day; also planted crops and cared for animals**

Overcoming Adversity • Book 6 — 75 — *Robinson Crusoe*

Chapter Quiz

Robinson Crusoe
Chapter 3, "A Footprint in the Sand"
Number the events in order from 1 to 5.

5 Several years passed before Crusoe saw another footprint.
2 Crusoe used animal skins to make a hat.
3 Crusoe was alone on the island for 11 years.
1 Crusoe built a canoe.
4 One day Crusoe found a human footprint.

Number the events in order from 6 to 10.

6 Through his spyglass Crusoe saw men dancing around a fire.
10 Crusoe called the man "Friday" and taught him English.
7 The men had two captives, but one of the captives escaped from them.
8 Crusoe fired his gun in the air as the captive ran toward him.
9 Crusoe smiled and signaled for the man to come forward.

Read the question, and write your answer.

Why does Crusoe say that the year he found Friday was his happiest year on the island? **Crusoe finally had human company.**

76 — Overcoming Adversity • Book 6 — *Robinson Crusoe*

82 — Overcoming Adversity • Book 6

Answer Key

Chapter Quiz

Name _____ Date _____

Robinson Crusoe
Chapter 4, "Two Others Join Us"
Fill in the bubble beside the answer for each question.

1. After Crusoe learned about the strange men on Friday's island, what did he plan to do?
   - (A) go to Friday's island
   - (B) go see the men who were there
   - ● both A and B

2. What did Friday say they needed to get to the island?
   - (A) a lot of food
   - ● a bigger boat
   - (C) both A and B

3. What kept Friday and Crusoe from starting their trip?
   - (A) wind
   - (B) hot sun
   - ● rain

4. Why would the other men on the island stay away from now on?
   - (A) They found other food.
   - ● They were afraid of the guns.
   - (C) Their canoes were wrecked.

Read the question, and write your answer.

How did Crusoe and Friday celebrate when they found Friday's father and the Spaniard? **made a big pot of goat soup**

Chapter Quiz

Name _____ Date _____

Robinson Crusoe
Chapter 5, "Rescued!"
Number the events in order from 1 to 5.

- **1** Using a spyglass, Crusoe saw an English ship sailing toward him.
- **4** The captain said Crusoe ruled the island.
- **5** Crusoe, Friday, the captain, and some sailors recaptured the ship.
- **2** Sailors brought three captives ashore.
- **3** When the sailors fell asleep, Friday and Crusoe set the captives free.

Number the events in order from 6 to 10.

- **8** Crusoe went back to Brazil.
- **6** Friday and Crusoe sailed to England.
- **9** In 1694 Crusoe visited the island.
- **7** Crusoe found out his plantation in Brazil had done well.
- **10** Friday stayed on the island when Crusoe left.

Read the question, and write your answer.

Why do you think Crusoe wanted to return to the island?
Ideas: see how things had changed, revisit place where he had lived for a long time

Chapter Quiz

Name _____ Date _____

Robinson Crusoe
Chapter 6, "Was Crusoe Real?"
Fill in the bubble beside the answer for each question.

1. Who may have been the real Crusoe?
   - (A) Daniel Defoe
   - ● Alexander Selkirk
   - (C) William Dampier

2. A *privateer* is a person who
   - ● is hired to recapture enemy ships.
   - (B) makes maps for the captain.
   - (C) steers the ship.

3. Dampier and Selkirk ended up in the
   - (A) Spice Islands.
   - ● Juan Fernández islands.
   - (C) Hawaiian Islands.

4. Selkirk became pilot of the
   - (A) *Weymouth*.
   - (B) *Cinque Ports*.
   - ● *Duke*.

Read the question, and write your answer.

Do you think *Robinson Crusoe* is fiction or nonfiction? Explain your answer.
Accept reasonable responses.

Thinking and Writing

Name _____ Date _____

Robinson Crusoe
Think About It
Write about or give an oral presentation for each question.

1. How did Crusoe feel when he saw the footprint in the sand? Why?
   Ideas: Crusoe was afraid; he was used to being alone.

2. What skills did Crusoe use to stay alive on the island? **Ideas: hunting, building, cooking, sewing**

3. Give some examples of foreshadowing from the story. **Idea: His parents warned him not to go to sea, and then he was shipwrecked.**

Write About It
Choose one of the questions below. Write your answer on a sheet of paper.

1. Crusoe was a survivor. What would you do to survive alone on an island? What would you do to keep from being bored?
2. Tell how this story fits the theme **Overcoming Adversity**. Give specific examples from the book.
3. Pretend you are Crusoe. Write a journal entry about one day on the island.
4. Complete the Book Report Form for this book.

Overcoming Adversity • Book 6

Building Background

Name _____ Date _____

Alice in Wonderland
What You Know

Write answers to these questions.

1. Do you usually remember your dreams after you wake up? Why do you think it's hard to remember them sometimes? _____
   _____

2. What kinds of things do you usually dream about? Why do you think you dream about those types of things? _____
   _____

3. How are your dreams the same as real life? _____
   _____

4. How are your dreams different than real life? _____
   _____

Word Meanings
Synonyms and Antonyms

Look for these words as you read your chapter book. When you find a word, write a synonym or antonym for the word.

Synonyms

excuse: _____

snout: _____

spiny: _____

Antonyms

angry: _____

awful: _____

uncomfortable: _____

Overcoming Adversity • Book 7

Word Lists

Alice in Wonderland

Unfamiliar Words	Word Meanings	Proper Nouns	
bored beautiful raisins ceiling gloves dodo	excuse		Chapter 1
nervous	angry	The Duchess	Chapter 2
disagreed height	awful	The Caterpillar	Chapter 3
terror noticed	snout	The Cheshire Cat The Hatter The March Hare	Chapter 4
court guests diamonds croquet arches flamingo hedgehogs straightened	spiny	The Dormouse	Chapter 5
judge jurors jury lessen nonsense taught trial verdict	uncomfortable	The Mock Turtle Tortoise	Chapter 6

Overcoming Adversity • Book 7

Chapter Quiz

Name _____ Date _____

Alice in Wonderland
Chapter 1, "Down the Rabbit Hole"

Mark each statement *T* for true or *F* for false.

_____ 1. Alice sees a rabbit with a watch.

_____ 2. Alice and her sister follow the White Rabbit down the hole.

_____ 3. When Alice lands, she finds a small gold key on a table.

_____ 4. Alice is too small to enter the garden behind the small door.

_____ 5. Alice drinks the contents of a bottle that is labeled, "Tea."

_____ 6. Alice grows big after eating a cake.

_____ 7. Alice makes a pool with her tears.

_____ 8. The Rabbit's watch makes Alice shrink.

_____ 9. Alice swims in her own tears.

_____ 10. The Rabbit gets caught in the pool of tears.

Read the question, and write your answer.

How does Alice interact with objects and characters in Wonderland?

_____

_____

_____

Chapter Quiz

Name _____ Date _____

Alice in Wonderland
Chapter 2, "A Long Tale"

Fill in the bubble beside the answer for each question.

1. After they swim in the pool of tears, how do the animals dry themselves?
    - Ⓐ They eat candy.
    - Ⓑ They stand in a circle.
    - Ⓒ They run a race.

2. The Mouse agrees to
    - Ⓐ tell a story.
    - Ⓑ give prizes.
    - Ⓒ share candy.

3. The animals begin to leave because Alice mentions
    - Ⓐ the Rabbit's fan.
    - Ⓑ her cat, Dinah.
    - Ⓒ the Mouse's tail.

4. What does the Rabbit order Alice to do?
    - Ⓐ drain the pool of tears
    - Ⓑ unknot the Mouse's tail
    - Ⓒ fetch a pair of gloves and a fan

Read the question, and write your answer.

What was the misunderstanding between Alice and the Mouse?

_____

_____

Overcoming Adversity • Book 7

Chapter Quiz

Name _____ Date _____

Alice in Wonderland
Chapter 3, "The Caterpiller's Advice"

Number the events in order from 1 to 5.

____ Alice says being three inches tall is awful.

____ The Caterpillar gets mad at Alice for her comment.

____ Alice says she doesn't know who she is.

____ Alice begins to walk away from the Caterpillar.

____ A blue caterpillar sitting atop a mushroom asks Alice who she is.

Number the events in order from 6 to 10.

____ Alice eats some of the mushroom and grows taller than the forest.

____ The Caterpillar tells Alice about the mushroom's growth properties.

____ Alice eats some of the mushroom and shrinks to less than one inch tall.

____ Alice eats some of the mushroom to get small enough to fit into a house.

____ Alice eats some of the mushroom and returns to her right size.

Read the question, and write your answer.

Why does Alice say she doesn't know who she is? _____

_____

_____

88   Overcoming Adversity • Book 7

Chapter Quiz

Name _____ Date _____

Alice in Wonderland
Chapter 4, "A Duchess"

Mark each statement *T* for true or *F* for false.

_____ 1. The Duchess, the Baby, and Alice sneeze because of dust in the air.

_____ 2. The Duchess says that the cat grins because it's a Cheshire Cat.

_____ 3. Alice likes that the Duchess called the Baby a pig.

_____ 4. The Cook throws pots, pans, and plates at the Duchess and the Baby.

_____ 5. The Duchess tells Alice not to touch the Baby.

_____ 6. The Baby turns into a pig.

_____ 7. The Cheshire Cat says everyone in Wonderland is mad.

_____ 8. The Cheshire Cat disappears and reappears.

_____ 9. The Cheshire Cat disappears until nothing is left but his tail.

_____ 10. Alice decides to visit the March Hare.

Read the question, and write your answer.

Why do you think the Baby changed into a pig? _____
_____
_____

Overcoming Adversity • Book 7

Chapter Quiz

Name _____ Date _____

Alice in Wonderland
Chapter 5, "A Party and a Game"

Fill in the bubble beside the answer for each question.

1. When Alice arrives, what are the Hare and the Hatter doing?
   - Ⓐ trying to put the dormouse into a teapot
   - Ⓑ having tea
   - Ⓒ setting the table for tea

2. What happened after the Hare had a fight with Time?
   - Ⓐ It's always six o'clock.
   - Ⓑ There is no time for tea.
   - Ⓒ They have time to wash the cups and plates.

3. Alice and the other characters play croquet with
   - Ⓐ mallets and balls.
   - Ⓑ eggs and arches.
   - Ⓒ flamingos and hedgehogs.

4. The croquet game did not go well for Alice because
   - Ⓐ the cards kept knocking her hedgehog out of bounds.
   - Ⓑ the Queen played a perfect game.
   - Ⓒ her flamingo kept curling its neck up.

Read the question, and write your answer.

What do you think will happen in the next chapter? _____

_____

_____

Chapter Quiz

Name _____ Date _____

Alice in Wonderland
Chapter 6, "A Turtle and a Trial"

Mark each statement *T* for true or *F* for false.

_____ 1. The Mock Turtle tells Alice about his teacher, Tortoise.

_____ 2. Alice hears a trial beginning, so she leaves the Turtle.

_____ 3. Alice thinks that the King looks very comfortable in his wig and crown.

_____ 4. The Jack of Hearts is on trial for stealing the Queen's jewelry.

_____ 5. As the first witness, the Hatter is so nervous that he bites his teacup.

_____ 6. Alice is not called as a witness.

_____ 7. The Queen argues that the sentence should come before the verdict.

_____ 8. Alice and the Queen become good friends.

_____ 9. The entire card pack flies toward Alice.

_____ 10. Alice wakes up and finds herself in a real courtroom.

Read the question, and write your answer.

What do you think Alice's sister will think about Alice's dream?

_____
_____
_____

Overcoming Adversity • Book 7

Thinking and Writing

Name _____ Date _____

Alice in Wonderland
Think About It

Write about or give an oral presentation for each question.

1. Think about Alice's character traits. Which character in Wonderland is most like Alice and why? Which is least and why? _____

   _____

   _____

   _____

2. Does Alice belong in Wonderland? Explain your answer. _____

   _____

   _____

3. How is Wonderland different than real life? _____

   _____

   _____

Write About It

Choose one of the questions below. Write your answer on a sheet of paper.

1. Alice's adventure begins when she falls down a rabbit hole. Write an original story about a character who enters another kind of animal home such as a bear's cave or a bird's nest.

2. Imagine you are Alice. Write a journal entry about your dream and how you felt about it. Include some of your interpretations on what you think different parts of the dream were about.

3. Complete the Genres Chart for this book.

Fluency Passages

Alice in Wonderland

Chapter 1 *page 3*

*Then Alice saw a little curtain. Behind the curtain was a small door.	13
The small gold key fit into the lock perfectly! Alice opened the little door.	27
She saw a beautiful garden on the other side. Alice really wanted to go into	42
that garden. But she was too big. She couldn't fit through the tiny door. So	57
she closed the door and locked it again.	65
She walked back to the glass table. On it was a bottle that hadn't been	80
there before. The bottle had a tag that read, "Drink Me." Alice drank from	94
the bottle. At first she didn't feel anything. Then she began to feel strange.	108
She looked at her hands. They were getting smaller. She was shrinking!	120
Soon she was only ten inches tall.	127
"What a curious* feeling," Alice thought.	133

Chapter 6 *pages 40 and 41*

**"Call the first witness," the King said. The first witness was the	12
Hatter. He had a cup in one hand and a piece of toast in the other. He didn't	30
look happy at all.	34
"Tell your story. And don't be nervous, or I'll cut off your head!" the	48
King yelled.	50
This did not help the Hatter one bit. He got so nervous that he took a	66
big bite out of his teacup! At that moment Alice began to feel very strange.	81
She was growing again!	85
The Hatter tried to explain about his never-ending tea party, even	96
though it didn't have anything to do with tarts or the Jack of Hearts.	110
"You may go," the King said when the Hatter was finished. "Call the	123
next witness!"	125
"Alice!" the Rabbit called. Alice* jumped up in surprise.	134

- The target rate for **Overcoming Adversity** is 130 wcpm. The asterisks (*) mark 130 words.
- Listen to the student read the passage. Count the number of words read in one minute and the number of errors.
- For the reading rate, subtract the number of errors from the total number of words read.
- Have students enter their scores on their **Fluency Graph.** See page 9.

Answer Key

Building Background

Name _____ Date _____

Alice in Wonderland
What You Know
Write answers to these questions.

1. Do you usually remember your dreams after you wake up? Why do you think it's hard to remember them sometimes? **Answers will vary.**

2. What kinds of things do you usually dream about? Why do you think you dream about those types of things? **Answers will vary.**

3. How are your dreams the same as real life? **Answers will vary.**

4. How are your dreams different than real life? **Answers will vary.**

Word Meanings
Synonyms and Antonyms
Look for these words as you read your chapter book. When you find a word, write a synonym or antonym for the word.

Synonyms
excuse: **forgive, pardon**
snout: **nose, muzzle**
spiny: **prickly, bristly**

Antonyms
angry: **pleased, delighted**
awful: **good, excellent**
uncomfortable: **relaxed, comfortable**

84 — Alice in Wonderland

Chapter Quiz

Name _____ Date _____

Alice in Wonderland
Chapter 1, "Down the Rabbit Hole"
Mark each statement *T* for true or *F* for false.

- **T** 1. Alice sees a rabbit with a watch.
- **F** 2. Alice and her sister follow the White Rabbit down the hole.
- **T** 3. When Alice lands, she finds a small gold key on a table.
- **F** 4. Alice is too small to enter the garden behind the small door.
- **F** 5. Alice drinks the contents of a bottle that is labeled, "Tea."
- **T** 6. Alice grows big after eating a cake.
- **T** 7. Alice makes a pool with her tears.
- **F** 8. The Rabbit's watch makes Alice shrink.
- **T** 9. Alice swims in her own tears.
- **F** 10. The Rabbit gets caught in the pool of tears.

Read the question, and write your answer.

How does Alice interact with objects and characters in Wonderland? **Ideas: experiments with the things she finds; tests the food and drink; tries to talk with the inhabitants**

86 — Alice in Wonderland

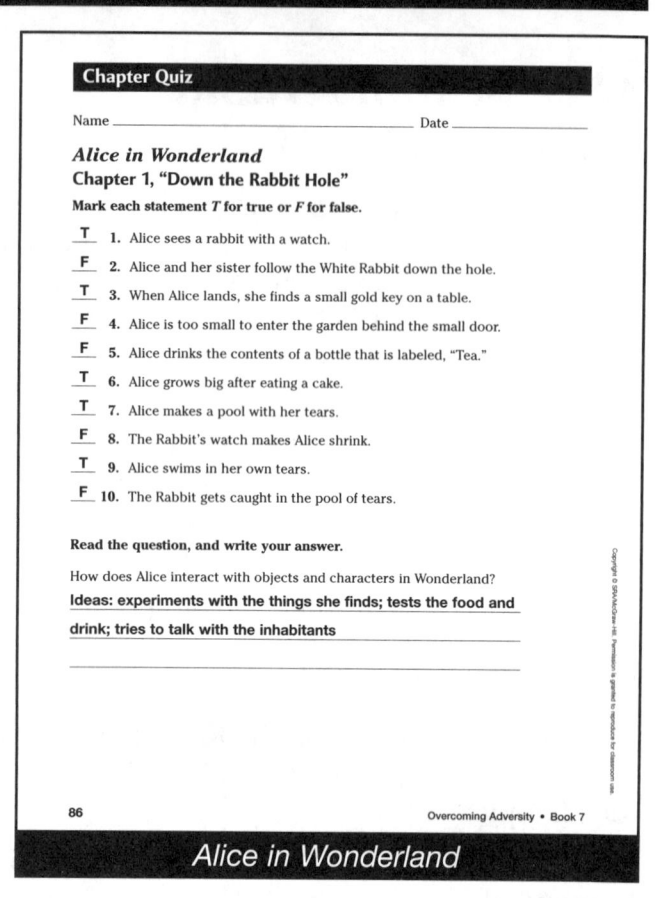

Chapter Quiz

Name _____ Date _____

Alice in Wonderland
Chapter 2, "A Long Tale"
Fill in the bubble beside the answer for each question.

1. After they swim in the pool of tears, how do the animals dry themselves?
   - Ⓐ They eat candy.
   - Ⓑ They stand in a circle.
   - ● They run a race.

2. The Mouse agrees to
   - ● tell a story.
   - Ⓑ give prizes.
   - Ⓒ share candy.

3. The animals begin to leave because Alice mentions
   - Ⓐ the Rabbit's fan.
   - ● her cat, Dinah.
   - Ⓒ the Mouse's tail.

4. What does the Rabbit order Alice to do?
   - Ⓐ drain the pool of tears
   - Ⓑ unknot the Mouse's tail
   - ● fetch a pair of gloves and a fan

Read the question, and write your answer.

What was the misunderstanding between Alice and the Mouse? **The Mouse wants to tell a *tale*, but Alice misunderstands the word *tale* to mean *tail* and focuses on the Mouse's *tail* rather than his *tale*.**

Overcoming Adversity • Book 7 — 87 — Alice in Wonderland

Chapter Quiz

Name _____ Date _____

Alice in Wonderland
Chapter 3, "The Caterpillar's Advice"
Number the events in order from 1 to 5.

- **4** Alice says being three inches tall is awful.
- **5** The Caterpillar gets mad at Alice for her comment.
- **2** Alice says she doesn't know who she is.
- **3** Alice begins to walk away from the Caterpillar.
- **1** A blue caterpillar sitting atop a mushroom asks Alice who she is.

Number the events in order from 6 to 10.

- **8** Alice eats some of the mushroom and grows taller than the forest.
- **6** The Caterpillar tells Alice about the mushroom's growth properties.
- **7** Alice eats some of the mushroom and shrinks to less than one inch tall.
- **10** Alice eats some of the mushroom to get small enough to fit into a house.
- **9** Alice eats some of the mushroom and returns to her right size.

Read the question, and write your answer.

Why does Alice say she doesn't know who she is? **Alice thinks that each change of size changes who she is or makes her a new person.**

88 — Alice in Wonderland

---

94 — Overcoming Adversity • Book 7

Answer Key

Chapter Quiz

Name _____ Date _____

Alice in Wonderland
Chapter 4, "A Duchess"
Mark each statement *T* for true or *F* for false.

- **F** 1. The Duchess, the Baby, and Alice sneeze because of dust in the air.
- **T** 2. The Duchess says that the cat grins because it's a Cheshire Cat.
- **F** 3. Alice likes that the Duchess called the Baby a pig.
- **T** 4. The Cook throws pots, pans, and plates at the Duchess and the Baby.
- **F** 5. The Duchess tells Alice not to touch the Baby.
- **T** 6. The Baby turns into a pig.
- **T** 7. The Cheshire Cat says everyone in Wonderland is mad.
- **T** 8. The Cheshire Cat disappears and reappears.
- **F** 9. The Cheshire Cat disappears until nothing is left but his tail.
- **T** 10. Alice decides to visit the March Hare.

Read the question, and write your answer.
Why do you think the Baby changed into a pig? **Accept reasonable responses.**

Alice in Wonderland

Chapter Quiz

Name _____ Date _____

Alice in Wonderland
Chapter 5, "A Party and a Game"
Fill in the bubble beside the answer for each question.

1. When Alice arrives, what are the Hare and the Hatter doing?
   - Ⓐ trying to put the dormouse into a teapot
   - ● having tea
   - Ⓒ setting the table for tea

2. What happened after the Hare had a fight with Time?
   - ● It's always six o'clock.
   - Ⓑ There is no time for tea.
   - Ⓒ They have time to wash the cups and plates.

3. Alice and the other characters play croquet with
   - Ⓐ mallets and balls.
   - Ⓑ eggs and arches.
   - ● flamingos and hedgehogs.

4. The croquet game did not go well for Alice because
   - Ⓐ the cards kept knocking her hedgehog out of bounds.
   - Ⓑ the Queen played a perfect game.
   - ● her flamingo kept curling its neck up.

Read the question, and write your answer.
What do you think will happen in the next chapter? **Accept reasonable responses.**

Alice in Wonderland

Chapter Quiz

Name _____ Date _____

Alice in Wonderland
Chapter 6, "A Turtle and a Trial"
Mark each statement *T* for true or *F* for false.

- **T** 1. The Mock Turtle tells Alice about his teacher, Tortoise.
- **T** 2. Alice hears a trial beginning, so she leaves the Turtle.
- **F** 3. Alice thinks that the King looks very comfortable in his wig and crown.
- **F** 4. The Jack of Hearts is on trial for stealing the Queen's jewelry.
- **T** 5. As the first witness, the Hatter is so nervous that he bites his teacup.
- **F** 6. Alice is not called as a witness.
- **T** 7. The Queen argues that the sentence should come before the verdict.
- **F** 8. Alice and the Queen become good friends.
- **T** 9. The entire card pack flies toward Alice.
- **F** 10. Alice wakes up and finds herself in a real courtroom.

Read the question, and write your answer.
What do you think Alice's sister will think about Alice's dream? **Ideas: will think the dream is strange; will be amazed by the detail and length of the dream**

Alice in Wonderland

Thinking and Writing

Name _____ Date _____

Alice in Wonderland
Think About It
Write about or give an oral presentation for each question.

1. Think about Alice's character traits. Which character in Wonderland is most like Alice and why? Which is least and why? **Ideas: Alice and the Cheshire Cat are similar because both are curious and change form; Alice and the Hare are most opposite because the Hare doesn't believe in logic and Alice does.**

2. Does Alice belong in Wonderland? Explain your answer. **Ideas: No, because she wants life to make sense. Yes, because she is curious about life and likes discovering Wonderland.**

3. How is Wonderland different than real life? **Ideas: Real life for Alice is normal, boring, or still, while Wonderland is unusual, exciting, and fluid.**

Write About It
Choose one of the questions below. Write your answer on a sheet of paper.

1. Alice's adventure begins when she falls down a rabbit hole. Write an original story about a character who enters another kind of animal home such as a bear's cave or a bird's nest.

2. Imagine you are Alice. Write a journal entry about your dream and how you felt about it. Include some of your interpretations on what you think different parts of the dream were about.

3. Complete the Genres Chart for this book.

Alice in Wonderland

Overcoming Adversity • Book 7

Building Background

Name _____ Date _____

Monte Cristo's Prison Years
What You Know

Write answers to these questions.

1. What does it mean to be jealous? Why would someone be jealous of another person? _____
_____

2. What is a trial? _____
_____

3. What is treason? Why would it be considered an especially offensive crime? _____
_____

4. How would you feel if no one believed what you were saying? How would you change their minds? _____
_____

Word Meanings
Matching

Look for these words as you read your chapter book. When you find a word, draw a line to connect the word with the correct definition.

abbot	an official elected or appointed to act as ruler
bier	a dark, usually underground, prison
dungeon	a person who helps the enemy of his or her country
francs	the head of a monastery for men
governor	a stand on which a coffin is placed
traitor	were once a basic unit of money in France

Overcoming Adversity • Book 8

Word Lists

Monte Cristo's Prison Years

	Unfamiliar Words	Word Meanings	Proper Nouns
Chapter 1	accept, arrest, comrade, fatal, guards, harbor, innocent, prison	governor, traitor	Count of Monte Cristo, Edmond Dantès, France, Frenchman, Marseilles [mahr-SAY], Mercédès, Villefort [veel-FAWR]
Chapter 2	government, impossible, swollen	abbot, dungeon, francs	
Chapter 3	continued, courage, dangerous, inspector, treasure, trial, violent		Abbot Faria, Toulouse [too-LOOZE]
Chapter 4		betray, continual, doubt, strength	Napoleon
Chapter 5		heir, refuses	Italy, Spada
Chapter 6		drew, remain	bier [BEERH]

Overcoming Adversity • Book 8

Chapter Quiz

Name _____ Date _____

Monte Cristo's Prison Years
Chapter 1, "The Prison"

Mark each statement *T* for true or *F* for false.

_____ 1. At first Dantès did not know where the guards were taking him.

_____ 2. Dantès was chained to the boat.

_____ 3. Dantès thought the letter had proof against him.

_____ 4. Dantès trusted Villefort because Villefort burned the letter.

_____ 5. Dantès was not loyal to France.

_____ 6. Dantès had committed a crime.

_____ 7. The boat was headed toward a prison.

_____ 8. Dantès promised not to escape and kept his promise.

_____ 9. Everything was clear to Dantès as he climbed the steps to the prison.

_____ 10. Dantès was given bread and water for dinner and fresh straw for a bed.

Read the question, and write your answer.

How do you think Dantès felt after realizing he was going to prison?

_____

_____

_____

Chapter Quiz

Name _____ Date _____

Monte Cristo's Prison Years
Chapter 2, "A Worse Place"

Fill in the bubble beside the answer for each question.

1. How did Dantès spend his first night in prison?
   - Ⓐ trying to escape
   - Ⓑ standing and weeping
   - Ⓒ sleeping soundly

2. What did Dantès want?
   - Ⓐ to see the governor
   - Ⓑ to eat better food
   - Ⓒ to move to a new cell

3. What happened to the abbot who had Dantès's cell before him?
   - Ⓐ He died.
   - Ⓑ He went mad.
   - Ⓒ He was set free.

4. What did Dantès ask the jailer to do for him?
   - Ⓐ help him escape
   - Ⓑ take a note to Mercédès
   - Ⓒ get him a better cell

Read the question, and write your answer.

What do you think Dantès wanted to write to Mercédès in the note?

_____

_____

Overcoming Adversity • Book 8

Chapter Quiz

Name _____ Date _____

Monte Cristo's Prison Years
Chapter 3, "The Two Prisoners"

Mark each statement *T* for true or *F* for false.

___ 1. Over a year passed before the inspector visited the prison.

___ 2. The prisoners told the inspector that the food was fine.

___ 3. The inspector cared about how the prisoners were treated.

___ 4. The inspector visited Dantès in the dungeon.

___ 5. Dantès begged to be shot if he were guilty of a crime.

___ 6. The inspector thought 17 months in prison was not very long.

___ 7. Dantès believed that Villefort was very kind to him.

___ 8. The Abbot Faria refused to share his treasure with the government.

___ 9. Dantès's records showed that he was innocent.

___ 10. The inspector arranged a trial for Dantès.

Read the question, and write your answer.

What does Faria promise the inspector? _____

_____

Chapter Quiz

Name _____ Date _____

Monte Cristo's Prison Years
Chapter 4, "Number 34 and Number 27"

Fill in the bubble beside the answer for each question.

1. What did Dantès decide to do after four years in prison?
   - Ⓐ dig a tunnel to the sea
   - Ⓑ starve himself
   - Ⓒ write letters to the newspapers

2. Dantès heard something in the middle of the night. What was it?
   - Ⓐ a scratching sound
   - Ⓑ a crying prisoner
   - Ⓒ dripping water

3. What did Dantès dig with?
   - Ⓐ a dinner fork
   - Ⓑ a pan handle
   - Ⓒ the jailer's sword

4. How did the other prisoner plan to escape?
   - Ⓐ go over the wall
   - Ⓑ steal keys from a guard
   - Ⓒ swim to an island

Read the question, and write your answer.

What do Dantès and the other prisoner discuss? _____

_____

Overcoming Adversity • Book 8   101

Chapter Quiz

Name _____ Date _____

Monte Cristo's Prison Years
Chapter 5, "The Treasure"

Mark each statement *T* for true or *F* for false.

_____ 1. Dantès and Faria met at night and planned their escape from prison.

_____ 2. Dantès taught Faria history and several languages.

_____ 3. Faria helped Dantès figure out who was to blame for putting him in prison.

_____ 4. Dantès decided to leave Faria behind because he was too sick to escape.

_____ 5. Faria told Dantès about a treasure.

_____ 6. Faria stole the money from the Spada family.

_____ 7. The Count of Spada had left his money to Faria.

_____ 8. Dantès wanted the money for himself.

_____ 9. Until he became ill, Faria did not plan to tell Dantès about the treasure.

_____ 10. Faria thought of Dantès as his son.

Read the question, and write your answer.

How do you think Dantès felt about his conversations with Faria?

_____

_____

Chapter Quiz

Name _____ Date _____

Monte Cristo's Prison Years
Chapter 6, "Escape"

Number the events in order from 1 to 5.

___ The guards put Faria's body in a canvas sack.

___ Faria told Dantès not to call for help even though he was dying.

___ The jailer found Faria dead and called for help.

___ Dantès heard someone calling him from Faria's cell.

___ Before he died, Faria told Dantès to hurry to Monte Cristo.

Number the events in order from 6 to 10.

___ Dantès got into the sack and sewed up the sack from the inside.

___ The men tied a weight to the sack and swung it to and fro.

___ Instead of burying the body, the men threw it into the sea.

___ Dantès took Faria's body out of the sack and moved it to his cell.

___ The men carried the sack outside the prison.

Read the question, and write your answer.

How do you think Dantès will free himself from the sack and the weight?

_____

_____

_____

Overcoming Adversity • Book 8

Thinking and Writing

Name _____ Date _____

Monte Cristo's Prison Years
Think About It

Write about or give an oral presentation for each question.

1. How do you think his years in prison changed Dantès? _____
   _____
   _____

2. Irony is the opposite of the expected outcome. Give some examples of irony from the story. _____
   _____
   _____

3. What do you think Dantès will do when he gets out of the sack?
   _____
   _____
   _____

Write About It

Choose one of the questions below. Write your answer on a sheet of paper.

1. The theme for these books is **Overcoming Adversity.** How did Dantès react at first? Who helped him to overcome adversity?

2. Pretend you are Dantès. Write a letter to Mercédès, telling her about life in the dungeon.

3. One element of this story is suspense. At the end of the story, things look hopeless for Dantès. But the introduction says Dantès becomes the Count of Monte Cristo. Write your own ending for this story.

4. Complete the Story Grammar Map for this book.

104   Overcoming Adversity • Book 8

Fluency Passages

Monte Cristo's Prison Years

Chapter 1 *pages 4 and 5*

*Dantès turned and saw they had gone out to sea. He turned to the	14
nearest guard. "Comrade," he said, "I beg you to tell me where we are	28
going. I am Captain Dantès, a loyal Frenchman. Tell me where you are	41
taking me. I promise you on my honor I will accept my fate."	54
Then a guard asked him, "You are from Marseilles and are a sailor,	67
and yet you do not know where you are going?"	77
"On my honor, I have no idea."	84
"Unless you cannot see, or have never been outside the harbor, you	96
must know," the guard said.	101
"I do not."	104
"Look round you."	107
Dantès rose and looked forward. Then he saw the black and frowning	119
rock on which the prison stands.	125
"The prison?" he cried. "Why* are we going there?"	134

Chapter 6 *page 36*

*Dantès could only clasp his hands and cry, "Oh, my friend, my	12
friend, do not speak this way!"	18
"There is no hope," Faria replied, shaking his head. "Now lift me onto	31
my bed, for I can no longer support myself."	40
Dantès took the old man in his arms and placed him on the bed.	54
"And now, my dear friend," Faria said, "I wish you happiness and	66
riches." The young man fell on his knees, leaning his head against the old	80
man's bed.	82
"Listen, now, to what I say," Faria said. "There really is a treasure. If	96
you do escape, remember that the poor abbot, whom all the world called	109
mad, was not so. Hurry to Monte Cristo. Find the treasure, for you have	123
suffered long enough." A violent fit attacked* the old man.	133

- The target rate for **Overcoming Adversity** is 130 wcpm. The asterisks (*) mark 130 words.

- Listen to the student read the passage. Count the number of words read in one minute and the number of errors.

- For the reading rate, subtract the number of errors from the total number of words read.

- Have students enter their scores on their **Fluency Graph.** See page 9.

Overcoming Adversity • Book 8

Answer Key

Building Background

Name _____ Date _____

Monte Cristo's Prison Years
What You Know

Write answers to these questions.

1. What does it mean to be jealous? Why would someone be jealous of another person? **Ideas: To be jealous is to want something that someone else has, like talents, friends, or money.**

2. What is a trial? **A *trial* is a court hearing held to decide if a person accused of a crime is innocent or guilty.**

3. What is treason? Why would it be considered an especially offensive crime? **betrayal of one's country; idea: treason can affect many people and put a country in danger**

4. How would you feel if no one believed what you were saying? How would you change their minds? **Ideas: frustrated, angry, hopeless; find proof, ask for help**

Word Meanings
Matching

Look for these words as you read your chapter book. When you find a word, draw a line to connect the word with the correct definition.

abbot — the head of a monastery for men
bier — a stand on which a coffin is placed
dungeon — a dark, usually underground, prison
francs — were once a basic unit of money in France
governor — an official elected or appointed to act as ruler
traitor — a person who helps the enemy of his or her country

96 — *Monte Cristo's Prison Years*

Chapter Quiz

Name _____ Date _____

Monte Cristo's Prison Years
Chapter 1, "The Prison"

Mark each statement *T* for true or *F* for false.

_T_ 1. At first Dantès did not know where the guards were taking him.
_F_ 2. Dantès was chained to the boat.
_T_ 3. Dantès thought the letter had proof against him.
_F_ 4. Dantès trusted Villefort because Villefort burned the letter.
_F_ 5. Dantès was not loyal to France.
_F_ 6. Dantès had committed a crime.
_T_ 7. The boat was headed toward a prison.
_F_ 8. Dantès promised not to escape and kept his promise.
_F_ 9. Everything was clear to Dantès as he climbed the steps to the prison.
_T_ 10. Dantès was given bread and water for dinner and fresh straw for a bed.

Read the question, and write your answer.

How do you think Dantès felt after realizing he was going to prison? **Ideas: confused, angry, scared**

98 — *Monte Cristo's Prison Years*

Chapter Quiz

Name _____ Date _____

Monte Cristo's Prison Years
Chapter 2, "A Worse Place"

Fill in the bubble beside the answer for each question.

1. How did Dantès spend his first night in prison?
   Ⓐ trying to escape
   ● standing and weeping
   Ⓒ sleeping soundly

2. What did Dantès want?
   ● to see the governor
   Ⓑ to eat better food
   Ⓒ to move to a new cell

3. What happened to the abbot who had Dantès's cell before him?
   Ⓐ He died.
   ● He went mad.
   Ⓒ He was set free.

4. What did Dantès ask the jailer to do for him?
   Ⓐ help him escape
   ● take a note to Mercédès
   Ⓒ get him a better cell

Read the question, and write your answer.

What do you think Dantès wanted to write to Mercédès in the note? **Ideas: He wanted to tell her that he had been wrongly imprisoned and ask for help to be set free.**

Overcoming Adversity • Book 8 99
Monte Cristo's Prison Years

Chapter Quiz

Name _____ Date _____

Monte Cristo's Prison Years
Chapter 3, "The Two Prisoners"

Mark each statement *T* for true or *F* for false.

_T_ 1. Over a year passed before the inspector visited the prison.
_F_ 2. The prisoners told the inspector that the food was fine.
_F_ 3. The inspector cared about how the prisoners were treated.
_T_ 4. The inspector visited Dantès in the dungeon.
_T_ 5. Dantès begged to be shot if he were guilty of a crime.
_T_ 6. The inspector thought 17 months in prison was not very long.
_T_ 7. Dantès believed that Villefort was very kind to him.
_F_ 8. The Abbot Faria refused to share his treasure with the government.
_F_ 9. Dantès's records showed that he was innocent.
_F_ 10. The inspector arranged a trial for Dantès.

Read the question, and write your answer.

What does Faria promise the inspector? **six million francs in exchange for his freedom**

100 — *Monte Cristo's Prison Years*

---

106   Overcoming Adversity • Book 8

Answer Key

Chapter Quiz

Name _____ Date _____

Monte Cristo's Prison Years
Chapter 4, "Number 34 and Number 27"
Fill in the bubble beside the answer for each question.

1. What did Dantès decide to do after four years in prison?
   - Ⓐ dig a tunnel to the sea
   - ● starve himself
   - Ⓒ write letters to the newspapers

2. Dantès heard something in the middle of the night. What was it?
   - ● a scratching sound
   - Ⓑ a crying prisoner
   - Ⓒ dripping water

3. What did Dantès dig with?
   - Ⓐ a dinner fork
   - ● a pan handle
   - Ⓒ the jailer's sword

4. How did the other prisoner plan to escape?
   - Ⓐ go over the wall
   - Ⓑ steal keys from a guard
   - ● swim to an island

Read the question, and write your answer.
What do Dantès and the other prisoner discuss? **Ideas: what Dantès is in the prison for; how Number 27 wants to escape**

Overcoming Adversity • Book 8   101

Monte Cristo's Prison Years

Chapter Quiz

Name _____ Date _____

Monte Cristo's Prison Years
Chapter 5, "The Treasure"
Mark each statement *T* for true or *F* for false.

- **T** 1. Dantès and Faria met at night and planned their escape from prison.
- **F** 2. Dantès taught Faria history and several languages.
- **T** 3. Faria helped Dantès figure out who was to blame for putting him in prison.
- **F** 4. Dantès decided to leave Faria behind because he was too sick to escape.
- **T** 5. Faria told Dantès about a treasure.
- **F** 6. Faria stole the money from the Spada family.
- **T** 7. The Count of Spada had left his money to Faria.
- **F** 8. Dantès wanted the money for himself.
- **F** 9. Until he became ill, Faria did not plan to tell Dantès about the treasure.
- **T** 10. Faria thought of Dantès as his son.

Read the question, and write your answer.
How do you think Dantès felt about his conversations with Faria?
Ideas: excited because it was something to look forward to; happy because he was learning

102   Overcoming Adversity • Book 8

Monte Cristo's Prison Years

Chapter Quiz

Name _____ Date _____

Monte Cristo's Prison Years
Chapter 6, "Escape"
Number the events in order from 1 to 5.

- **5** The guards put Faria's body in a canvas sack.
- **2** Faria told Dantès not to call for help even though he was dying.
- **4** The jailer found Faria dead and called for help.
- **1** Dantès heard someone calling him from Faria's cell.
- **3** Before he died, Faria told Dantès to hurry to Monte Cristo.

Number the events in order from 6 to 10.

- **7** Dantès got into the sack and sewed up the sack from the inside.
- **9** The men tied a weight to the sack and swung it to and fro.
- **10** Instead of burying the body, the men threw it into the sea.
- **6** Dantès took Faria's body out of the sack and moved it to his cell.
- **8** The men carried the sack outside the prison.

Read the question, and write your answer.
How do you think Dantès will free himself from the sack and the weight?
Accept reasonable responses.

Overcoming Adversity • Book 8   103

Monte Cristo's Prison Years

Thinking and Writing

Name _____ Date _____

Monte Cristo's Prison Years
Think About It

Write about or give an oral presentation for each question.

1. How do you think his years in prison changed Dantès?
   Ideas: Dantès learned a lot from Faria; he will not be as trusting as he was before.

2. Irony is the opposite of the expected outcome. Give some examples of irony from the story. **Ideas: Dantès tells the inspector to believe what Villefort wrote; Dantès prepares to be buried, not drowned.**

3. What do you think Dantès will do when he gets out of the sack?
   Ideas: He will go to Monte Cristo to get the treasure; he will get revenge.

Write About It

Choose one of the questions below. Write your answer on a sheet of paper.

1. The theme for these books is **Overcoming Adversity**. How did Dantès react at first? Who helped him to overcome adversity?

2. Pretend you are Dantès. Write a letter to Mercédès, telling her about life in the dungeon.

3. One element of this story is suspense. At the end of the story, things look hopeless for Dantès. But the introduction says Dantès becomes the Count of Monte Cristo. Write your own ending for this story.

4. Complete the Story Grammar Map for this book.

104   Overcoming Adversity • Book 8

Monte Cristo's Prison Years

Overcoming Adversity • Book 8   107

Graphic Organizer

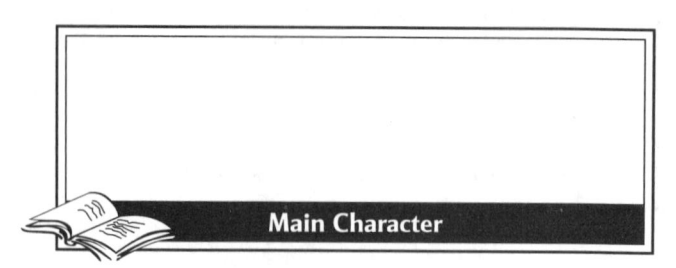

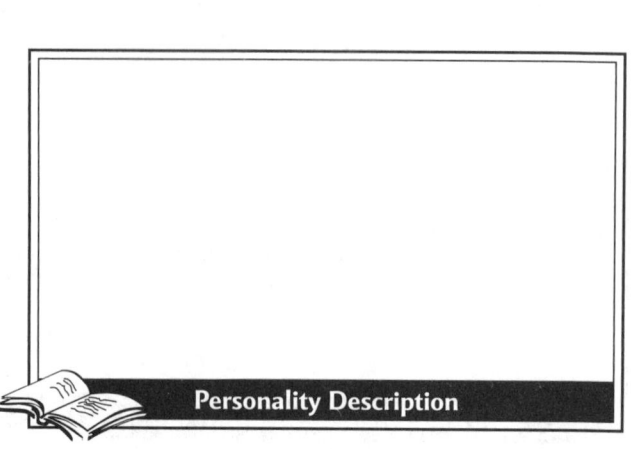

Name _____ Date _____

The Last Boat
Book Report Form

Describe the main character from your book by writing descriptions in the boxes as needed.

Main Character

Physical Description

Personality Description

Early Life

Influential People

Achievements

Significant Events

Overcoming Adversity

Graphic Organizer

Name _____ Date _____

Inspiring Excellence
Cause and Effect Chart

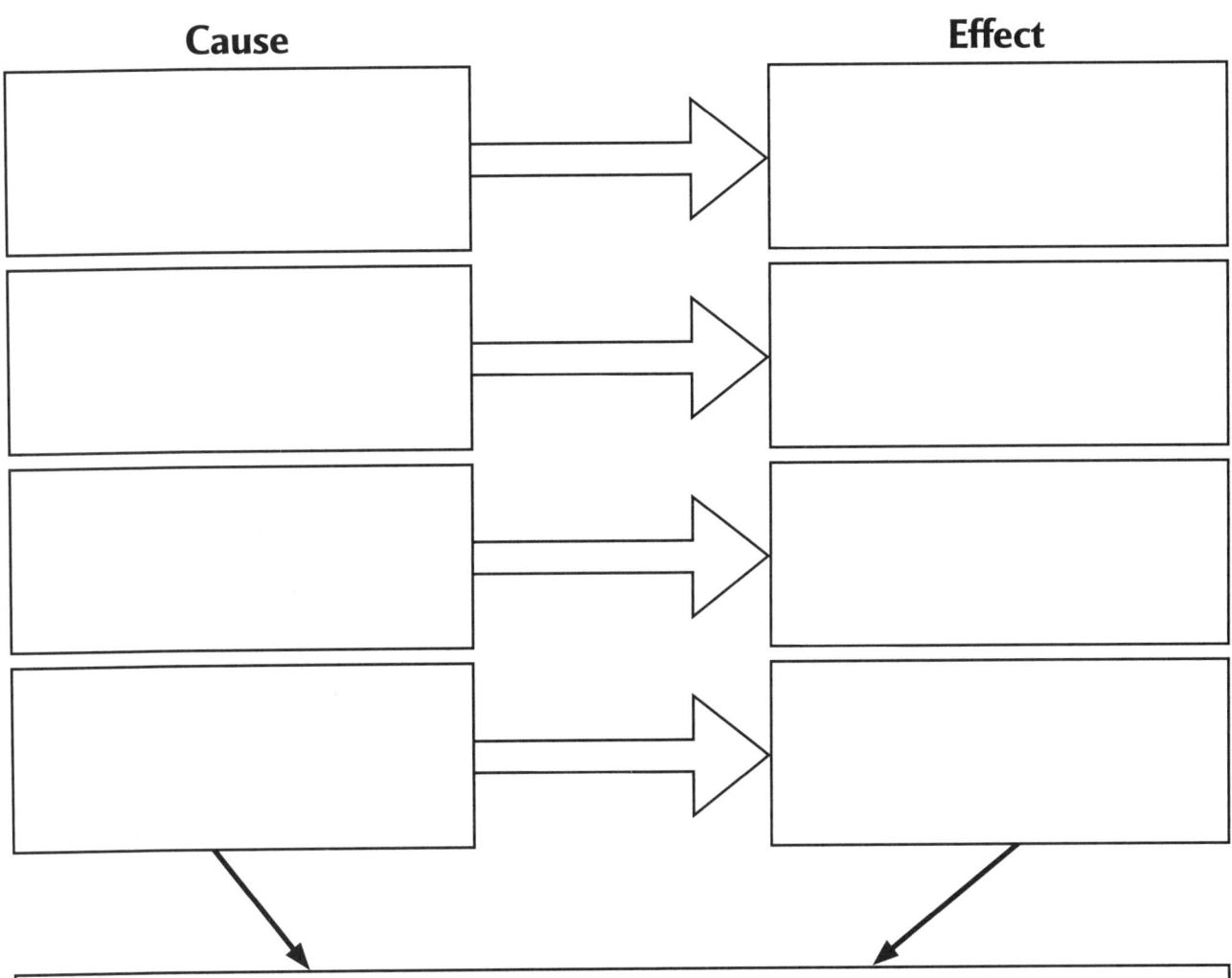

Cause → **Effect**

- Explain how you think each of the athlete's disabilities have changed them and helped them aspire to excellence.
- Do you think these athletes would have pushed themselves to become excellent in their chosen sports without their disabilities? Why or why not?

Overcoming Adversity

Graphic Organizer

Name _____ Date _____

Playing through Pain
What I Know/What I Learned Chart

What I Know	What I Want to Know	What I Learned

Graphic Organizer

Name _____ Date _____

Once There Were Two
Content Web

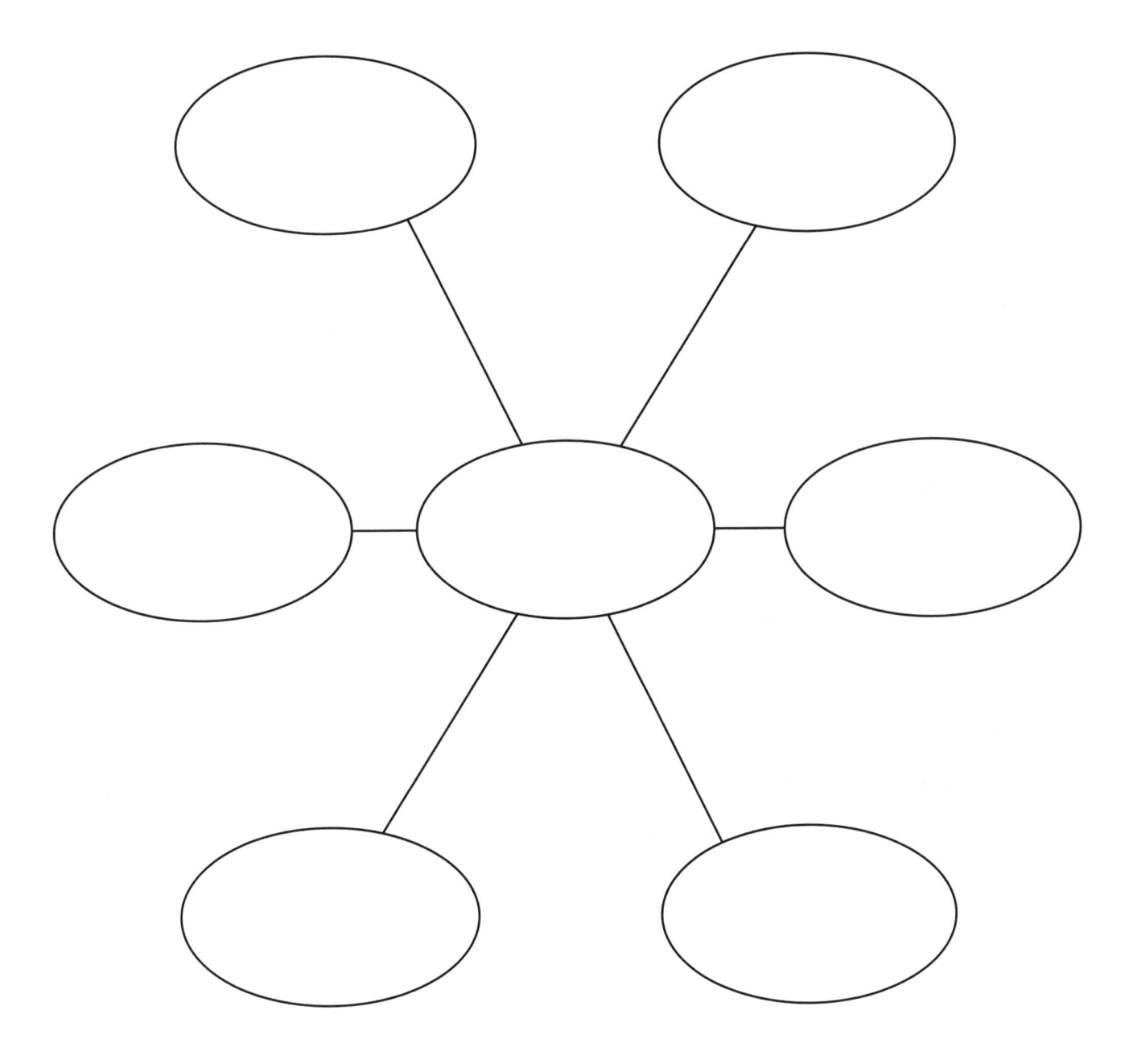

Overcoming Adversity

111

Graphic Organizer

Name _____ Date _____

Walls of Water
Compare and Contrast Diagram

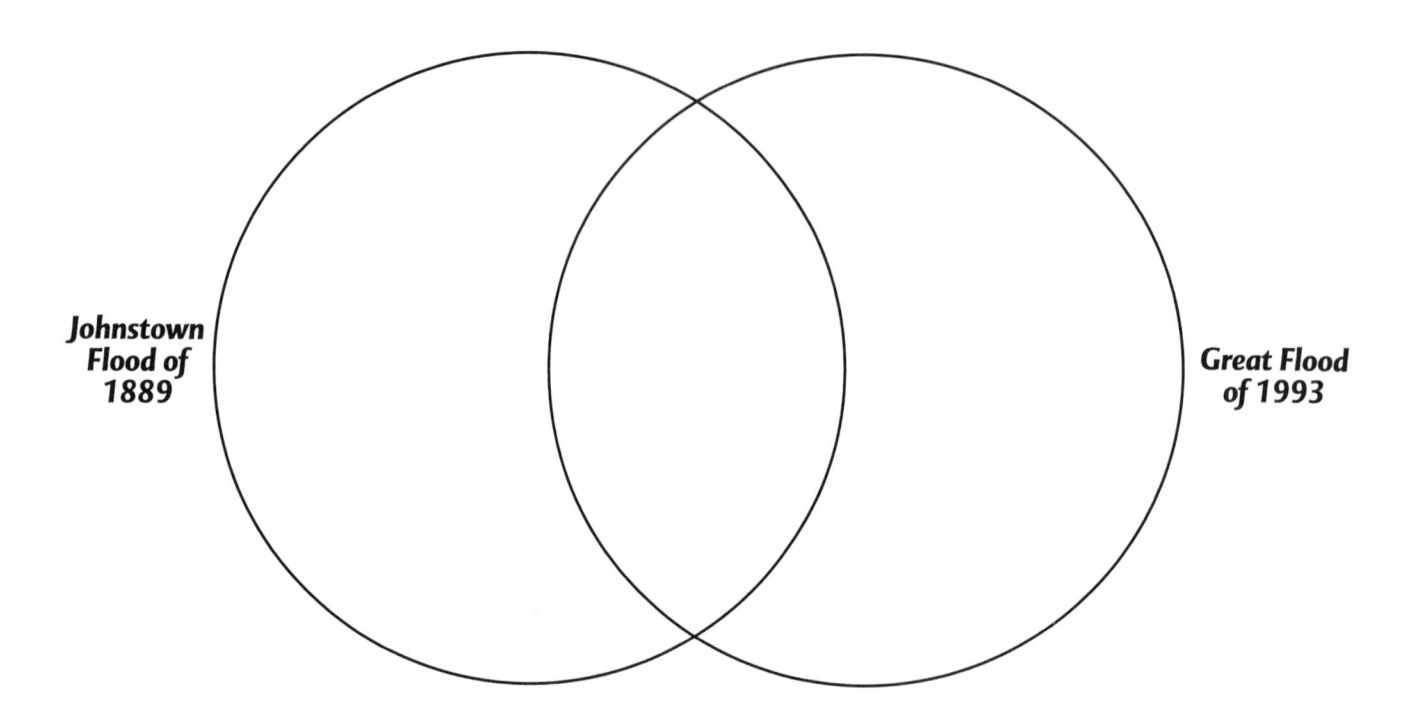

Johnstown Flood of 1889

Great Flood of 1993

- What is **different** about the Johnstown Flood of 1889 goes in the circle on the left.
- What is **different** about the Great Flood of 1993 goes in the circle on the right.
- What is the **same about both** goes in the overlapping area in the middle.

112

Overcoming Adversity

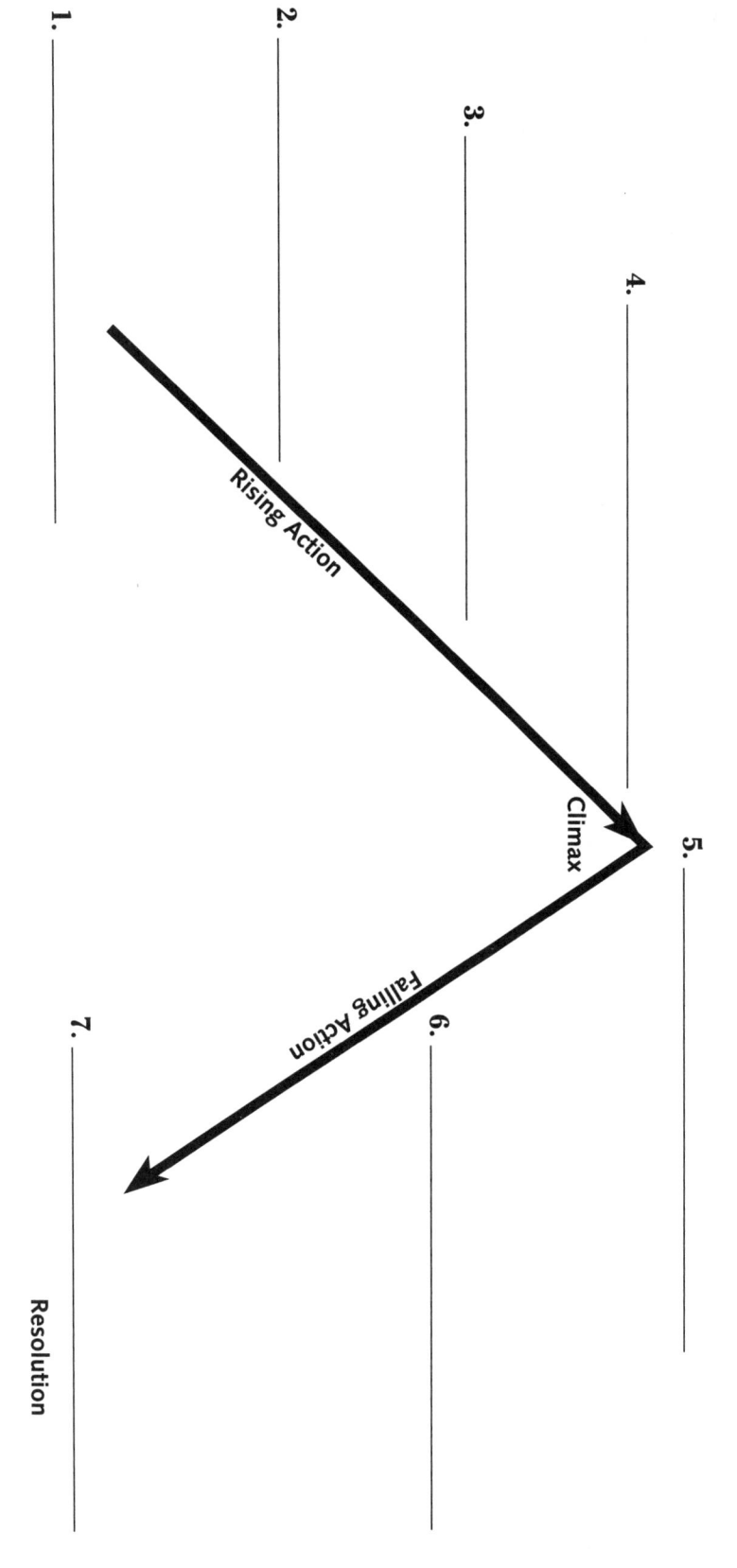

Graphic Organizer

Name _____ Date _____

Robinson Crusoe
Book Report Form

On lines 1–4, list the major plot events. On line 5, write the turning point or climax of the conflict. On line 6, write the falling action. On line 7, write how the story ended.

1. _____

2. _____

3. _____

4. _____

Rising Action

Climax

5. _____

Falling Action

6. _____

7. _____

Resolution

Overcoming Adversity

Graphic Organizer

Name _____ Date _____

Alice in Wonderland
Genres Chart

Reality (fact)	Fantasy (fiction)

Overcoming Adversity

Graphic Organizer

Name _____ Date _____

The Count of Monte Cristo
Story Grammar Map

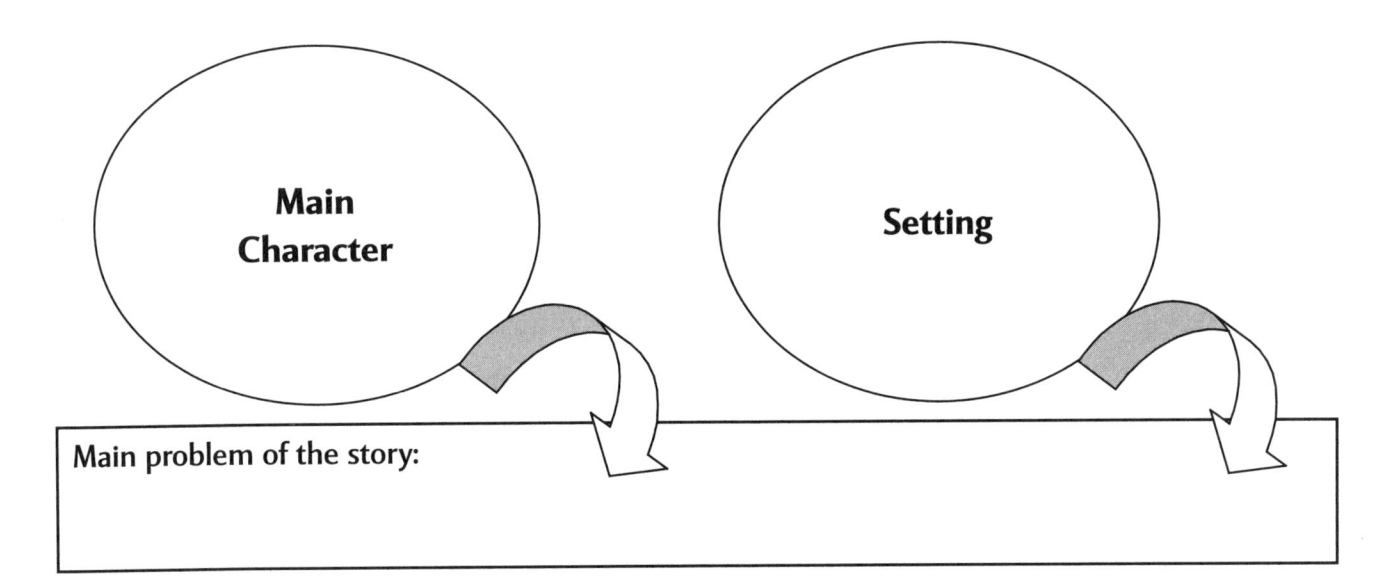

(Main Character)   (Setting)

Main problem of the story:

An event in the story:

An event in the story:

How was the story's problem solved?

What is the ending?

Overcoming Adversity